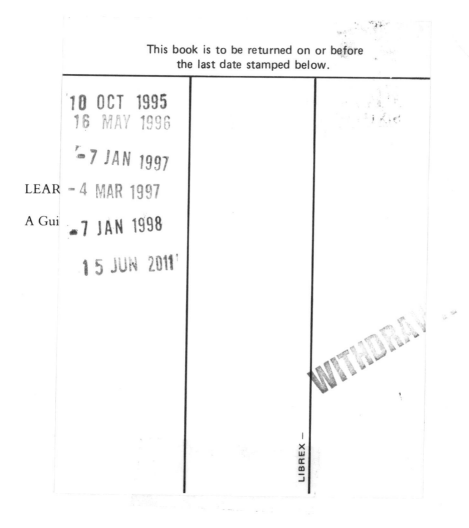

LEARNING HISTORY
A Guide to Advanced Study

Richard Brown
Previously Head of History,
Houghton Regis Upper School, Bedfordshire

Christopher W. Daniels
Culford School, Suffolk
Sometime Schoolmaster Fellow Commoner,
Sidney Sussex College, Cambridge

MACMILLAN

First published 1986 by
MACMILLAN PRESS LTD
Houndmills, Basingstoke, Hampshire RG21 2XS
and London
Companies and representatives
throughout the world

ISBN 0–333–38650–7

A catalogue record for this book is available
from the British Library.

15   14   13   12   11   10   9   8   7
03   02   01   00   99   98   97   96   95

Printed in Malaysia

To the students of Houghton Regis Upper School and to Matthew, Neal, Jason, Duncan, Philip, Tim, Udo, Tania, Wendy and Helen and many other RLS historians

Contents

Acknowledgements

Christopher Daniels would like to thank: The Master and Fellows of Sidney Sussex College, Cambridge, for offering a Schoolmaster Fellow Commonership during which much of this book was written; Professor Ivan Roots of Exeter University for the Sackville Crowe material; Mr Richard Abbey of Guildford for valuable comments on the typescript from the viewpoint of a recent 'A' level historian; Mr John Mills of Thornborough, Buckingham (now of Lincoln) for the material from Thornborough census 1851, using his commercially available computer program from Mills Historical and Computing; staff and pupils of Culford School, Suffolk, for continuing advice up to publication, especially the Headmaster, Mr Derek Robson, colleagues in the History Department, sixth-form historians and the gentle criticisms of the Upper Fifth of Edwards House; and most of all Vanessa Peerless for guiding this book through all its stages, and constant encouragement from the Macmillan Press.

The authors and publishers wish to thank the following who have kindly given permission for the use of copyright material: Collins Publishers for the extract from *Undertones of War* by Edmund Blunden: Longman Group Ltd for the extracts from *The Scramble for Africa* by M. E. Chamberlain (1974); P. R. Newman for 'Marston Moor, 2nd July 1644: The Sources and the Site', in *Borthwick Papers*, no. 53 (1978); Routledge & Kegan Paul plc for the extract from *The Origins of Modern English Society 1780–1880* by H. Perkins (1969).

The authors and publishers also wish to acknowledge the following illustration sources: By gracious permission of Her Majesty the Queen – 5.2; The Mansell Collection – 3.1, 5.3, 5.9; Buckinghamshire County Archive – 5.11; Buckinghamshire Archaeological Society – 5.12, 5.13; Manchester City Council – 3.2, 3.3; The British Library – 5.4, 5.5; *Punch* – 5.7; *The Standard* – 5.6, 5.8.

Every effort has been made to trace all the copyright holders but if any have been inadvertently overlooked the publishers will be pleased to make the necessary arrangements at the first opportunity.

Preface

The transition from courses leading to an examination at 15 or 16 plus to a course with an examination at 18 plus can be an awkward leap: not only may the period of history be different, but the type of work may change, demanding a wider range of more specialised books and articles, more complex documentary work, essays needing increased use of analytical skills, more emphasis on debate, greater self-reliance at home and in private study sessions, and so on.

Even for a gifted student these changes can be daunting, and for most students – especially if history is a new subject – the first few months can be full of stress. The high point of 16 plus examination success in the summer may soon fade under the pressure of new courses or transfer to another school or college.

This book is designed to be read and used by student historians in the sixth form and in the first year of higher education courses. It is not a manual for instant success, nor is it a revision guide or compendium for any particular syllabus. Examples have been selected from a wide range of course options from the sixteenth to the twentieth century, including British, European and world history. Any bias towards particular centuries or regions indicates the most popular courses according to student numbers in examinations. Do not be put off an example because it falls outside your course. The lessons to be learned from all the examples will have some bearing on problems or topics within your period.

The book opens with a chapter on *How to Start*. This is crucial because it is often a worrying time at the beginning of a new course. Suggestions are made on interesting books to use when starting a course, simple ideas on time-charts to build up a sense of period and chronology, how to become involved with the period being studied and the making of notes. Clearly, teachers and tutors will help considerably – the book is no replacement for them – but there are several pointers on how to get the most out of the course from the outset.

Chapter 2 investigates the writing of essays, a major requirement in all courses and examinations at this level and beyond. A late-seventeenth-century example is taken in depth, and examples of student writing are offered for analysis and criticism. The chapter provides no highway to first-class essays, but offers guidance on what is expected and how it may be achieved. It ends with a guide by L. G. Brandon to the different wording and types of examination questions.

Documentary material in various forms – written, printed, visual and oral – is playing a more significant role in courses for 16- to 19-year-old students than previously, so three chapters are assigned to studying it. Chapter 3 is an introduction to evidence, using as a case-study the 'Peterloo Massacre' of 1819, with many opportunities for understanding how historians approach and use evidence.

Chapters 4 and 5 look at the variety of evidence. Chapter 4 takes two themes – *Political Parties and Elections, 1689–1714* and *The Scramble for Africa, c. 1870–1914* – and explores several aspects of them, using primary written or printed sources with questions that involve comprehension, analysis and synthesis.

Chapter 5 looks into the rich vein of visual, statistical and oral evidence. Again, the emphasis is placed on studying the variety of sources and the questions to be asked of them by the historian. The range is broad, encompassing examples from the Tudors to the twentieth century: from woodcuts to the computer.

Secondary sources are covered in Chapter 6, which describes how to tackle the kind of books commonly used at this level. These range from popular history through biographies to more specialised monographs. The art of extracting information easily and quickly from long and detailed books is of enormous value both at this stage and in a future occupation.

Chapter 7 illustrates the fascinating theme of historical debates by offering brief discussions on three important and challenging examples. As Christopher Haigh wrote, debates are to the historian what experiments in the laboratory are to the scientist. The three debates are:

British history: Elizabethan Parliaments
European history: The Origins of the First World War
                    The Social and Economic Effects of the Thirty Years'
                    War on Germany

Suggestions are made on how to take part in the debates and on further reading and thought.

The final chapter looks beyond the syllabus into broader aspects of the study of history: What *is* history? What are the links between history and other disciplines? What other aspects of history are there beyond the political, diplomatic and economic issues so familiar in examination papers? These other aspects may be the springboard for deeper involvement in the subject, perhaps through a research project.

The book concludes with a select list of useful books on the study of history, which should be readable at age 16 to 19.

We hope that these chapters will enable students of a wide range of ability to begin and continue courses at 16–19 level with confidence and success. As already mentioned, the book is no substitute for a teacher or tutor, but whether used as a group text or for personal guidance we hope that it will be of value in the changing world of courses and examinations at this level. The authors welcome views, criticism and suggestions from students and their teachers on this book, and may be contacted through the publishers.

RICHARD BROWN
CHRISTOPHER W. DANIELS

1 How to Start

History, Jonathan Steinberg wrote, should be fun. 'If history is not fun it is not for you. Find yourself another subject.' How should the student historian attain this enjoyment? Interest and involvement may be developed and sustained by a variety of approaches, many of which take place outside the school or college: four of these are books, television, film and visits.

Books

By their very nature textbooks are not usually the most exciting way of entering an historical period: 'of making many books there is no end; and much study is a weariness of the flesh'! So why not try an historical novel? Some of these are classic works of literature, for example Stendhal's *Le Rouge et le Noir* or Balzac's *Le Père Goriot* (available in translation) on early nineteenth-century France, but many popular ones are still *based* on historical fact, and it is a useful exercise to try to separate fact from fiction. Here is an example on the reign of James I:

(a) Nigel Tranter

King James had turned round to face the bridge again, and was pointing, arm and finger still trembling from his alarm and emotion. He spoke thickly – always he spoke thickly, wetly, for his tongue was too large for his mouth and the spittle ran constantly down his straggly beard, as adequate an excuse for a permanent thirst as might be devised. To steady himself, he grabbed Sir Charles Percy's richly padded sleeve, with the other hand.

'Yon's a right shameful brig,' he declared. 'Your brother, this Northumberland, should have done better for me, man. It's no' right and proper, I tell you. I . . . we are much disappointed. Yon's a disgrace. We might have been submerged in the cruel waters – aye, submerged. It wabbles, sirs – it quakes. It'll no' do, I say.'

'To be sure, Sire. As your Majesty says. But I assure Your Majesty that it is safe. Entirely safe.' Northumberland, still clutching the as yet undelivered address of welcome from the Privy Council in London, was earnestly placatory. 'It has always been thus. I have ridden across it a hundred times . . .'

'It shoogles, sir – it shoogles. And creaks. Are you contesting my royal word, Englishman?'

'No, Sire – no! I swear! But . . . but . . .'

The Bishop gallantly, if rashly, came to the rescue. 'Your Majesty, old wooden bridges *do* creak. In especial long ones. And, er, quiver somewhat. But it has survived a thousand storms . . .'

'Each more weakening it, man – weakening it. Guidsakes, you came here, to bide *this* side, waiting on me, *me* your prince, to take his life in his two hands, and cross yon death-trap to you! What like a people and nation is this I've come amongst?'

'But, Highness – this *is* the English side. Where it was our duty, our joyful duty, to wait and greet you. On setting your royal foot on our, h'm, on *your* English soil. For the first time, Berwick Bridge, therefore, is only half in this realm of England. Your Majesty will not hold us responsible for, for the Scots end . . .?'

'Na, na, mannie – you'll no' win awa' with that sort o'talk, see you. Yon ill Richard Plantagenet stole Berwick from us lang-syne; 1427 to be precise – aye, 1427, nigh on two centuries past. You've sat snug in our Berwick since then, have you no'? Complain as we would. *North* o' the brig. So you'll no can jouk your responsibilities. *Incidis in Scyllam cupiens vitare Charybdim.* You, a churchman, will ken what that means?'

'Er, yes, Sire.' Tobias Mathew was as unused to a monarch as quoted Latin at him, as he was to one who gabbled in almost incomprehensible dialect, dribbled and prayed to his Maker in the public highway. He sought to change the subject. 'We have letters for Your Majesty. From the Convocation of Canterbury and York, and from the High Council of Parliament. And, of course, Your Majesty's Privy Council . . .'

'Aye. But this brig,' the King said. 'It'll no' do. You'll just hae to build a new one. D'you hear? My command – aye, our first royal command on this our English ground. A guid new stout brig o'stone, see you. That'll no' wabble. Forthwith. See you to it, my lords. My . . . my Treasury in London will pay for it.'

There was a moment of utter silence.

(*The Wisest Fool – A Novel of James the Sixth and First*, N. Tranter, Coronet edn, 1974, pp. 10–11)

Another readable author of historical fiction is Thomas Flanagan, whose *Year of the French* (1979) was dramatised on television's Channel 4. The book describes the frustrated hopes of Ireland during the French invasion of 1798.

Some novels were written by people actively involved in the politics of their time: the Victorian statesman Benjamin Disraeli, Earl of Beaconsfield, wrote several novels. This extract is from *Sybil or the Two Nations* (1845) set at the time of the Chartist troubles of the 1830s:

(b) Benjamin Disraeli

'Come, don't you preach,' said the Chartist. 'The Charter is a thing the people can understand, especially when they are masters of the country; but, as for moral force, I should like to know how I could have marched from Wodgate to Mowbray, with that on my banner.' . . .

At this moment a great noise sounded without the room, the door was banged, there seemed a scuffling, some harsh high tones, the deprecatory voices of many waiters. The door was banged again, and this time flew open, while, exclaiming in an insolent coarse voice, 'Don't tell me of your private rooms; who is master here, I should like to know?' there entered a very thickset man, rather under the middle size, with a brutal and grimy countenance, wearing the unbuttoned coat of a police sergeant conquered in fight, a cocked hat, with a white plume, which was also a trophy of war, a pair of leather breeches and topped boots, which from their antiquity had the appearance of being his authentic property. This was the leader and liberator of the people of England. He carried in his hand a large hammer, which he had never parted with during the whole of the insurrection. . . . 'They won't [he said] stop the works at the big country mill you were talking of. They won't, won't they? Is my word the law of the land or is it not? Have I given my commands that all labour should cease till the Queen sends me a message that the Charter is established, and is a man who has a mill to shut his gates upon my forces, and pump upon my people with engines? There shall be fire for this water. . . .'

'Trafford is a humane man,' said Morley in a quiet tone, 'and behaves well to his people.'

'A man with a big mill humane! . . . with two or three thousand slaves working under the same roof, and he doing nothing but eating their vitals. I'll have no big mills where I'm main master. Let him look to it. Here goes,' and he jumped off the table. 'Before an hour I'll pay this same Trafford a visit, and I'll see whether he'll duck me.' . . . nodding to the Chartist to follow him, the Liberator left the room.

Hatton turned his head from the window, and advanced quickly to Morley. 'To business, friend Morley. This savage cannot be quiet for a moment; he exists only in destruction and rapine. If it were not Trafford's mill, it would be something else. I am sorry for the Traffords; they have old blood in their veins. Before sunset their settlement will be razed to the ground. Can we prevent it? Why not attack the castle instead of the mill?'

(Benjamin Disraeli, *Sybil or the Two Nations*, World's Classics edn, 1926, pp. 397–400)

Contemporary diaries are equally readable: Samuel Pepys and John Evelyn are well known commentators on late seventeenth-century England. Here is Evelyn on the restoration of Charles II in 1660:

(c) John Evelyn

[1660] 29*th* [May] This day, his Majesty, Charles the Second came to London, after a sad and long exile and calamitous suffering both of the King and Church, being seventeen years. This was also his birth-day, and with a triumph of above 20,000 horse and foot, brandishing their swords, and shouting with unexpressible joy; the ways strewed with flowers, the bells ringing, the streets hung with tapestry, fountains running with wine; the Mayor, Aldermen, and all the Companies, in their liveries, chains of gold, and banners; Lords and Nobles, clad in cloth of silver, gold, and velvet; the windows and balconies, all set with ladies; trumpets, music, and myriads of people flocking, even so far as from Rochester, so as they were seven hours in passing the city, even from two in the afternoon till nine at night.

I stood in the Strand and beheld it, and blessed God. And all this was done without one drop of blood shed, and by that very army which rebelled against him: but it was the Lord's doing, for such a restoration was never mentioned in any history, ancient or modern, since the return of the Jews from their Babylonish captivity; nor so joyful a day and so bright ever seen in this nation. . . .

6*th*. [July] His Majesty began first to *touch for the evil!* according to custom, thus: his Majesty sitting under his state in the Banqueting-house, the chirurgeons cause the sick to be brought, or led, up to the throne, where they kneeling, the king strokes their faces, or cheeks with both his hands at once, at which instant a chaplain . . . says, 'He

put his hands upon them, and he healed them.' . . . then the Lord Chamberlain and
the Comptroller . . . bring a basin, ewer and towel, for his Majesty to wash.

(*The Diary of John Evelyn* ed. W. Bray, Everyman edn, 1952, pp. 341, 343)

Carlo Levi was punished for his opposition to the Fascists by being exiled
to a remote part of southern Italy. His account of this exile is a masterpiece on
the social and economic problems of Italy since unification, and of the nature
of Fascism:

(d) Carlo Levi

There were a great number of speeches at this time and Don Luigi was zealous in
calling public meetings. It was October and our troops had crossed the Mareb; the war
with Abyssinia had begun. Italians, arise! America receded ever more into the
distance, lost in the mists of the Atlantic like an island in the sky.

The peasants were not interested in the war. . . . So the 'fellows in Rome' wanted
war and left it up to the peasants to do the fighting? All well and good. It couldn't be
much worse to die in an Abyssinian desert than to perish from malaria in a pasture by
the Sauro river. It seemed that schoolchildren and their teachers, Fascist Scouts, Red
Cross ladies, the widows and mothers of Milanese veterans, women of fashion in
Florence, grocers, shopkeepers, pensioners, journalists, policemen, and government
employees in Rome, in short, all those generally grouped together under the name of
'Italian people', were swept off their feet by a wave of glory and enthusiasm. Here
in Gagliano I could see nothing. The peasants were quieter, sadder, and more dour
than usual. . . . The 'fellows in Rome' didn't usually put themselves out on their
behalf. . . .

'If they have money enough for a war, why don't they repair the bridge across the
Agri which has been down for four years without anyone moving a finger to fix it?
They might make a dam or provide us with more fountains, or plant young trees
instead of cutting down the few that are left. . . .'

War they considered just another inevitable misfortune, like the tax on goats. They
were not afraid to go . . . but [few] enlisted. . . .

'The war is for the benefit of those in the north. We're to stay home until we starve.
And now there's no chance of going to America'.

(*Christ Stopped at Eboli*, Carlo Levi, Penguin edn, 1982, pp. 130–2)

Reading books like these will be more enjoyable and more profitable than
relying solely on a textbook for inspiration and excitement, or struggling
with a monograph, which may be only the latest contribution to a complex
and difficult debate. (Books of that nature have a vital historical function but
they can be left for the moment.)

History Today is a monthly magazine whose issues contain good short
articles which concentrate on interesting aspects or events over the whole
span of human history. They do not avoid controversial twentieth-century
themes and there are many well chosen illustrations. Try to read articles
outside the period that you are studying, as history is concerned with breadth
as well as depth. Read the book reviews as well. They offer insights into a
book and its author, but they should also inform on historical criticism, the
state of research in that area and the personality of the reviewer.

Television and Film

The visual counterpart to *History Today* is the BBC TV programme *Timewatch*, where three or four items are investigated each month. These are usually topical and highly visual, and they introduce academic historians specialising in the topic, although not all of these come across equally well in front of the cameras. Channel 4 also offers stimulating history programmes, including two in recent years on the history of Scotland and Wales. The latter was fortunate in its two presenters, both of whom had different historical explanations for many of the key events in the history of Wales, and were not afraid to demonstrate and argue them!

Many of the Open University history programmes are compelling viewing; a good example was *A203 Seventeenth-Century England: A Changing Culture* which linked politics, society and the arts, with superb programmes on architecture.

Film is an even more contentious medium than historical fiction, as examples like *Cromwell* or *The Charge of the Light Brigade* show, but can often capture a mood, and the best films go even further. Olmi's *The Tree of Wooden Clogs*, set in late nineteenth-century rural Italy, was a superb evocation of peasant life.

Visits

Visits to archaeological sites and buildings of historical interest encourage understanding of what it meant to live in a certain place at a certain time. The following are examples:

Grimes Graves, Norfolk (Neolithic flint mines)
Hadrian's Wall
Jorvik exhibition, York
Durham Cathedral
City of York
Fountains Abbey, Yorks.
Bodiam Castle, Sussex
Lavenham church, Suffolk
Battlefield of Bosworth, Leics.
Little Moreton Hall, Cheshire
Knole, Kent
Royal Naval College, Greenwich
Castle Howard, Yorks.
Stowe, Bucks.
H.M.S. Victory, Portsmouth
Quarry Bank Mill, Styal, Cheshire
Carlton Towers, Yorks.

Gladstone Pottery Museum, Stoke-on-Trent
Cabinet War Rooms, London
Castle Drogo, Devon

Historic Houses, Castles and Gardens, published annually by British Leisure Publications, has a wealth of examples. There is a companion volume on museums.

In each case the mood, the atmosphere, is as important as the particular details of architecture or ornament. How does one recognise that Little Moreton is sixteenth-century, much of Knole early seventeenth, Castle Howard early eighteenth, Carlton Towers nineteenth and Castle Drogo twentieth? It is made possible by the ability to recognise features relating to a certain period of history and to avoid anachronism. The same applies to art, music, literature and technology. As Jonathan Steinberg wrote, 'Had Sir Ian Hamilton, General Monash and General Stopford been supplied with three walkie-talkie sets, the British Gallipoli offensive [1915] would have succeeded and the First World War, and possibly world history, would have been changed.' (This and further Steinberg quotes from R. Bennett (ed.), *First Class Answers in History*, Weidenfeld & Nicolson, 1974)

All of these aspects – books, television, film and visits – should help in the development of an historical imagination. Maurice Powicke referred to 'held reverberations' when he visited historic sites, 'the sense of a conscious past'. Perhaps this may be discerned in the popular books of G. M. Trevelyan, of whom George Kitson Clark wrote that 'he could paint a scene, he could tell a story and he could describe a man.'

Chronology

A useful aid in developing chronology and making sense of a new period being studied is to draw up an outline of events – political, social, economic, cultural – based on your reading. The following example is a start and a few textbooks now offer chronological guides (see A. G. R. Smith, *The Emergence of a Nation State, 1529–1660*, Longman 1984, pp. 3–9, 221–32). These can be particularly valuable in reminding the historian that 'domestic', 'foreign', 'social' and other thematic groupings of events often occurred at the same time, not in isolation from each other. As Maurice Powicke wrote, 'Social life loses half its interest and political movements lose most of their meaning if they are considered apart.' Change in one theme may have taken place at a different rate than in another but contemporaries did not necessarily separate them in practice: religion, domestic politics and foreign affairs were inextricably interlinked for many seventeenth-century Englishmen, while inhabitants of Britain during the Industrial Revolution did not separate economic changes from politics, as the Chartist movement demonstrates.

(a) Chronological table

1603 Elizabeth d. (March 24); the King of Scotland becomes K. as JAMES I.

1604 Present authorized translation of Bible begun (completed, 1611).
The Hampton Court Conference, between the bishops and Puritans.
Peace made with Spain.

1605 The Gunpowder Plot discovered (Nov. 5).
Barbados colonized by the English (the oldest British colony).

1606

1607 Parliament refuses to grant free trade between England and Scotland, but repeals the border laws.
The Ulster chiefs O'Neill and O'Donnell flee to Spain, and James confiscates the land belonging to their tribes.

1608 The Virginia Company makes the first permanent English settlement in America.
Birth of John Milton.

1609

1610 Parliament presents Petition of Grievances.
Plantation of Ulster by English and Scottish settlers begins.

1611 James I dissolves his first Parliament for not meeting his wishes. He institutes the order of Baronets to raise money.

1612 Death of Robert Cecil, Earl of Salisbury (May).
Death of Henry, Prince of Wales (Nov.)
Establishment of Episcopacy in Scotland.

1613 Marriage of the King's daughter Elizabeth to Frederic, Elector Palatine.

1614 Meeting and dissolution of second Parliament (Apr.–June); known as the *Addled Parliament*.

1615

1616 Dismissal of Chief Justice Coke, for resisting the King.
Death of Shakespeare.
George Villers (afterwards D. of Buckingham) becomes favourite of the King.

1617 Negotiations opened with Spain for marriage of Prince Charles with the Infanta.

1618 Execution of Sir Walter Raleigh, nominally for treason, in reality to please Spain.
General Assembly of Scotland passes the Articles of Perth.

1619

1620 Landing of the Pilgrim Fathers in New England.

(*Time Table of Modern History AD 400–1870*, M. Morison, 1908)

Historical novels and so on make the subject more enjoyable and help to evoke the 'spirit of the age', but for most students, the textbook and lecture will be *the* basic media through which history will be learnt. The last section of this chapter deals with the fundamental skill of note-taking.

Taking Notes

Historians use words a great deal either in spoken or written form. The ability to extract the central points or arguments from lectures or books is therefore a skill of major importance. Although there are differences between taking notes from lectures and from books students often perceive note-taking in one of two ways. On the one hand there are those individuals who find note-taking a pointless chore. To them the whole process is mechanical and without any real value or stimulus. On the other hand there are those individuals who treat notes as 'Holy Writ'. Their approach is best illustrated by the following:

> I walked into an Upper Sixth History lesson this afternoon and said, 'Good afternoon.' Four students looked up, three responded and six wrote it down just in case they missed something.

This method is uncritical, unthinking and as wasteful as the first approach. In neither case have the students actually thought about why they are taking notes.

It is important to have the following two points clear when note-taking. First, notes are for you, nobody else. Although some notes may be examined, and sometimes marked, by your teachers they are part of your thinking and reflection on a particular subject. They should be written *only* for you as triggers and aids to learning. Secondly, there is little point in taking notes on anything unless they are solidly based on your understanding of that subject. Unless there is some understanding then you will hardly be able to make useful and intelligible notes on it. In this sense 'intelligible' means that you will be able to understand the notes when you return to them tomorrow, in a month or in a year's time. Taking notes is a highly individual activity: whether the method used actually works is the only criterion of success.

Lectures

Lectures are essentially a one-way communication process. The lecturer talks and you listen, but this should not be a passive process. Lectures should guide your thoughts and emphasise the basic essentials as well as the more complex and easily misunderstood aspects of a subject. They should draw attention to different interpretations and should bring new work to your attention. They should stimulate your thinking and subsequent learning. They should complement your reading. Lewis Carroll wrote:

'I think I should understand that better,' Alice said very politely, 'if I had it written down: but I can't quite follow it as you say it.'

It is easy to lose the thread of a lecture. Your mind can easily wander, so taking notes can aid your concentration.

It is impossible and undesirable to reproduce the contents of a lecture exactly. Your notes should be a consciously selected version of the material offered. It is important to find a balance between listening and recording information and ideas. Sometimes the teacher will help you by using phrases like 'the following four points are central to the argument' or 'It is important to note that'. Listening is therefore as important as writing if your notes are to be discriminating and critical.

One approach to note-taking is the sequential or linear method. In this approach students record:

(a) the main points made by the lecturer or teacher in numerical order;
(b) each main point is accompanied by concise summaries of supporting detail and examples;
(c) enough explanation to provide continuity between the main points;
(d) any statement, quotation etc. dictated by the teacher is copied down;
(e) any additional source of information mentioned in the lecture.

Below is an example of linear notes on the state of religion in the mid-eighteenth century:

NOTES — STATE OF ANGLICAN RELIGION IN MID-XVIII CENTURY
(1) Analysis of organisational structure of C of E –
    (a) the provinces;
    (b) the diocese;
    (c) the parishes.
(2) Parallel to these three structural divisions were three levels within the hierarchy of personnel in the Church –
    (a) the archbishops;
    (b) the bishops;
    (c) the priests – advowson, glebe, tithe.
    Reference: for 1 and 2 see appendix in R. K. Webb; *Modern Britain*.
(3) C of E as established church; deeply embedded in framework of national life; imp of relationship between pol. and eccl estab.
    (a) financial basis of the church;
    (b) Thirty-Nine Articles 1562 – document open to latitude of interpretation; 1662 Act of Uniformity;
    (c) Church and education – notion of social control;
    (d) 1689 Toleration Act – importance and constraints;
    (e) imp of theory of Church and State (Erastian): England a single civil and religious society – implications for dissenters;

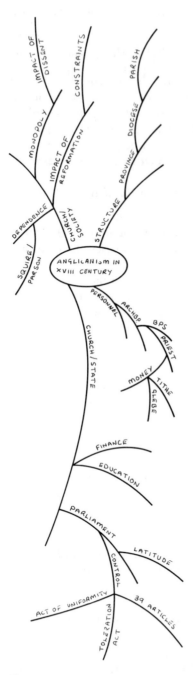

Figure 1.1

(f) inc criticism of Ch from early XVIII century – 'latitudinarianism' under attack.

(4) Relationship between society and religion?
  (a) result of Reformation and Tudor/Stuart legislation;
  (b) dependence of Church on State;
  (c) weakness of monopolistic pretensions of Anglicanism.

'Industrialism, political change and a complex of accompanying developments in the social structure would all place pressures upon the values and beliefs of society.'

These notes should provide the foundation upon which your understanding can be built. As soon as possible after the lecture you should review your notes. Do you understand everything you have written? Do you need to edit your notes further so they reflect the lecture more accurately? Do you need to expand your notes to reflect reading suggested in the lecture? Lectures are not an end in themselves but a means to understanding. Since they are usually a one-way process, using and discussing your lecture notes with fellow students is essential if you want to understand them more fully.

An alternative to this sequential approach is called either the 'creative pattern method' or 'creative doodling' or 'mind maps'. Rather than starting from the top of the page and working down in sentences and lists you should start from the central or main idea and then branch out (Figure 1.1). This approach has certain advantages over the sequential approach. The central or main idea is more clearly defined. The importance of the idea is clearly indicated: the more important ideas are nearer to the centre with the less important ones nearer the edge. This approach allows the student to establish the relationship between the key concepts and will aid recall. The sequential notes above can be shown creatively.

To assist you in the process of note-taking and understanding, consider the following questions:

(1) Compare the linear and creative methods of making notes from lectures. Which one do you prefer and why?
(2) What do you get out of lectures? How can effective note-taking help you to improve your understanding of the subject?
(3) How does the identification of 'key-words' help you in developing your ideas about the past?

Books and the written word

The major difference between taking notes from lectures and taking them from the written word is that there is more time for reflection. The student can use different coloured pens to emphasise points. First, these emphases may help to identify structure, the central ideas and crucial information. Secondly, the author's purposes and assumptions, either implicit or explicit, can be made clear. Finally, they allow the student to identify points which need to be followed up. Consider the following passage:

What is more, problems which are acute in modern underdeveloped countries setting about their industrialization were mild in eighteenth-century Britain. As we have seen, transport and communications were comparatively easy and cheap, since no part of Britain is further than seventy miles from the sea, and even less from some navigable waterway. The technological problems of the early Industrial Revolution were fairly simple. They required no class of men with specialized scientific qualifications, but merely a sufficiency of men with ordinary literacy, familiarity with simple mechanical devices and the working of metals, practical experience and initiative. The centuries since 1500 had certainly provided such a supply. Most of the new technical inventions and productive establishments could be started economically on a small scale and expanded piecemeal by successive addition. That is to say, they required little initial investment, and their expansion could be financed out of accumulated profits. Industrial development was within the capacities of a multiplicity of small entrepreneurs and skilled traditional artisans. No twentieth-century country setting about industrialization has, or can have, anything like these advantages.
This does not mean that there were no obstacles in the path of British industrialization, but only that they were easy to overcome because the fundamental social and economic conditions for it already existed, because the eighteenth-century type of industrialization was comparatively cheap and simple, and because the country was sufficiently wealthy and flourishing to be untroubled by inefficiencies

which might have crippled less fortunate economies. Perhaps only so lucky an industrial power as this could have ever afforded that distrust of logic and planning (even private planning), that faith in the capacity to muddle through, which became so characteristic of Britain in the nineteenth century.

(E. J. Hobsbawm, *Industry and Empire*, Pelican, 1969, pp. 39–40)

(1) Examine this passage in relation to the three points of emphasis made above.
(2) What are the 'keywords' in this passage?
(3) Produce linear and creative notes for this passage. Compare them.

An important part of studying history in the sixth form and beyond is that the opportunities for learning independently increase. This involves studying on your own initiative, making decisions about how and when to work. Lessons or classes will provide you with a framework in which to study. Your teachers may well indicate what they want you to do in 'study periods', but you will still need to consider the following questions:

What am I studying and in what depth or breadth?
How shall I approach the topic? Are the lesson notes sufficient? What additional material do I need?
How is the work to be evaluated?
How much time should I spend on this study?
With whom will I discuss my work?

History is often seen as a passive subject. The student does not actually do anything positive other than produce essays, usually from secondhand material. This may be less true today than a few years ago with documentary and project work now taking on an increasing importance, but as Thomas à Kempis wrote 600 years ago: 'When the day of judgement comes, we shall not be asked what we have read, but what we have done.'

2 The History Essay

The Uses and Value of the Essay

History depends on good communication, so clarity in written work is essential. What *is* good written work and how can the historian improve his skills?

The three main forms of historical writing are narration, description and analysis:

(1) Narration involves chronology – the placing of an event or sequence of events within a time scale. One event follows another, though not necessarily caused by it, and this is part of the uniqueness of history.

(2) Description is used less in advanced essays, but it has an important function at times; a description of the events of January 1933 does much to explain why and how Hitler came to power.

(3) Analysis is the most important of the three: why did an event take place, what difference did it make, and what consequences were there?

These questions are the essence of history at 'A' level and beyond, and distinguish the good student from the mediocre. An essay will usually include a blend of all three aspects, as we shall see later in the chapter, but first here are some items relating to a seventeenth-century member of the gentry, Sir Sackville Crowe.

The information has been collected fortuitously by Professor Ivan Roots of Exeter University. His view is that Crowe was not a major figure but is worth remembering as an example of the opportunities and problems met by careerists. Crowe certainly finds no place in the multi-volume *Dictionary of National Biography*. The aim is to write an interesting biography based on the evidence, attempting to describe and explain his career as you might find it in a textbook. Your answer should be about 1,200 words long.

b. about 1600 at Brasted, near Sevenoaks, Kent, of minor gentry family with kin in Kent and Sussex.
d. 1680 at Laugharne, Carmarthen, S. Wales, where he had had estates and interests since the 1630s.
A private secretary to the Duke of Buckingham in the early 1620s; keeps the Duke's privy purse, records of gambling debts, tips, etc; goes on the trip to Madrid, 1623, where Prince Charles woos the Infanta.

In the late 1620s secures a Baronetcy.

Treasurer of the Navy; makes about £1,000 a year in fees, perquisites, etc. [N.B. For most offices the salary was a minor part of the reward, which could extend to influence, patronage, patents of monopoly, etc.] After his departure, the Chatham Chest – a fund for the relief of distressed mariners – was found to be somewhat attenuated!

One of several agents of Charles I on the Continent pawning some of the royal jewels in the late 1620s.

M.P. for Bramber, Sussex, in 1628–9 Parliament.

Enters marriage market and competes with Dr Raven and Sir John Finch – 'birds of a feather'! – for a rich city widow. Loses! Later marries into the Manners family.

In the 1630s a Patentee for the supply of iron ordnance from the Weald of Kent and Sussex; also involved in the Forest of Dean.

An 'undertaker' for fen draining in Carmarthenshire. Buys property there and sets up family seat. Seeks and maintains contacts and interests in local politics.

'Ambassador' in Turkey in the 1630s; difficulties with the Levant Company who find him rapacious and meddlesome. Agent for Archbishop Laud's collection of Persian miniatures and manuscripts.

Portrait painted by native artist – since disappeared.

With the Civil War, was put in the Tower by the Long Parliament at the behest of the Levant Company. Produced pamphlets on trade; one included a scheme for the revival of something like Henry VII's *Malus Intercursus*. Controversy with William Walwyn, the Leveller, who had his own schemes for commercial reform, especially against monopolistic trading companies.

Crowe was described in Parliament (1656–8) as 'this extravagant person' whose 'proceedings seem to be black and dark enough' (Burton's *Diary*).

Released in 1660. Claims his constant loyalty to the monarchy, and, like many others, expects a reward from Charles II. Presents petitions and proposals 'for the public good' to the King.

Assigned control of the Mortlake tapestry works for his and the nation's interest. Competition from the Netherlands and France (Gobelins) proved too strong. Crowe relinquished it in 1667 as a losing concern and therefore of no appeal to him, though in giving it back to the King he says he does so 'only out of a jealousy and care that so excellent an ornament to the nation might not suffer by my hand'.

Spends more time now in Carmarthen. Sometime mayor of the town. Involved in parliamentary election manoeuvres, the sort of thing for which by character, temperament, experience and expectation he was well fitted. Local people appeal to him for support in getting jobs, etc. A schoolmaster wanting to set up a school in Carmarthen mentions Crowe's 'discreet moderation . . . [and] gentle disposition'!

1677, made a Patentee of the office of Clerk of the Court to the revived Council in the Marches of Wales: has power to appoint, etc., thereby reinforcing his influence, prestige, income, etc.

But in spite of that falls on hard times, and dies a debtor in the Fleet Prison.

His son, Sackville, second Baronet, died without issue. Baronetcy extinct.

This material was arranged in no particular order, was often ungrammatical, and made very little attempt to explain aspects of Crowe's varied career. Since one of the purposes of history is to obtain order from chaos, then consider these extracts from essays written, like your own, using this material and making good sense of it. What are their strengths and weaknesses?

(A) Both the Tudors and Stuarts placed much of their trust in 'self-made' men. These were opportunists, who did not come from prominent noble families, but had made their own way to wealthy positions. After reaching these positions they tried to gain the patronage of established noblemen or even the Royal family. However, they did not own any land and were, therefore, excluded from the nobility. In order to establish themselves and their families, they spent much of their wealth on estates and frequently took part in local affairs.

Sir Sackville Crowe, born c. 1600, was a good example of a self-made man. He began in the early 1620's as the private secretary to the Duke of Buckingham. His career was not, however, a smooth progression. At its high points Crowe was Treasurer of the Navy, Ambassador in Turkey, in control of the Mortlake Tapestry works and Clerk of the Court to the revived Council of the Marches of Wales; at its low points he was imprisoned in the Tower by the Long Parliament, he was referred to as 'this extravagant person' whose 'proceedings seem to be black and dark enough' (Burton's Diary) and, according to one source, he died a debtor in Fleet Prison. . . .

[Sixth paragraph] Despite all these marvellous achievements Crowe did have several low points in his career. His first was in 1629 after he had been an M.P. for Bramber in Sussex. This Parliament had been the one which introduced the Petition of rights and other resolutions against the Church and the State. It is impossible to say whether Crowe supported these measures, but he does not take an active part in Charles administration for some years after 1629. It was in his capacity as Ambassador in Turkey, that Sackville made the enemies which were to cause his next downfall. He interfered continually with the Levant Company. This company had held an Elizabethan Charter, allowing them to be sole traders with Asia via Turkey. When they surrendered the Charter they were still allowed to take duties from importers of currants and other such merchandise. Thomas Smyth, who was a very important figure in the London financial circles, had a large interest in Levant. It was probably through his pressure that the Long Parliament placed him in the Tower. . . .

[Conclusion] Sir Sackville Crowe was a good example of a Stuart age 'self-made' man. He had a fairly humble start in life as the son of a minor gentleman, but during his life his career led him to many foreign places, he took part in some of the major actions in his lifetime. He survived through three monarchs, a civil war and a Commonwealth. He was a survivor and that was important at that time, but he was more because he was an adventurer as well. This led to his downfall sometimes, but most of the time it was this spirit of adventure which made him a successful careerist.

(B) [Penultimate paragraph] Although he held positions of importance some of Crowe's dealings were very dubious. After he left his position of treasurer of the Navy the Chatham Chest which was a fund for the relief of distressed Mariners, was found to be somewhat empty. While in Parliament Crowe was described as 'this extravagent person' whose 'proceedings seem to be black and dark enough'. Even after his release from the Tower of London in 1660 he claimed his constant loyalty to the Monarchy and expected rewards from Charles II. Crowe would obviously do anything for money and prestige and he even entered the marriage market, trying to find a rich widow. He did not manage this and later married into the Manners family.

How does your version compare with these? The first essay has an assertive introduction (indicating background knowledge of the period), and considers most of the evidence. Do you agree with the arrangement of the material, the conclusions drawn from the evidence, and the amount of background information in the introduction and sixth paragraph? Does the conclusion add anything different from the introduction? How effective is the sentence construction and paragraph design? What is the balance between narration, description and analysis?

Note how the single paragraph of the second essay places some of Crowe's financial aspects together. Is this thematic treatment better than straight chronology? Are the generalisations too broad?

As you can see, there are several possibilities in tackling historical writing, and a good essay requires more than accuracy of grammar and factual information, important though these are.

John Kentleton of Liverpool University argued the values of the essay in the following ways:

(1) Its ability to encourage cogency of argument. The essay writer is obliged to move beyond the mere statement of fact. Intellectually, he is obliged to strike out for deep water. One cannot tackle a subject piecemeal; if the essay is to succeed it requires an overall view and perception. Each statement requires an ensuing one. Each statement has to be examined for its inherent validity and for its relative validity to the whole.

(2) Its training in logic. . . . There is nothing like having to arrange an argument on paper to tauten one's thoughts; nothing like reading such an argument to spot at leisure the inconsistencies and half-truths that lie hidden within it. . . . It is mentally healthy not to be able to jump across the river wearing the seven-league boots of a set of assumptions, but to have to construct an intellectual suspension bridge, the weakness of any one part of which will bring the whole edifice crashing into the torrent below.

(3) The encouragement it gives to critical analysis; its extended treatment of a subject allows space and time for the ruthless stripping bare of a subject. Why is the statement faulty? Why is this evidence suspect? Why is such an argument questionable? . . . [The writer] learns that if he cannot always give the correct answers, he can ask the correct questions . . . not just . . . acquire information but . . . use it, examine it and render it malleable to [his] intellectual strength. . . .

(4) Its training in the assignment of emphasis. . . . It is the ability not only to see essentials but to give just weight and consideration to lesser factors; to see the wood notwithstanding the trees, yet remember there are trees of all sorts of shapes and sizes. . . . One reason why examiners are right to penalize the paper that provides the three and a bit answers for the four that are requested, is because the candidate has failed to learn one of the salient lessons of his training; that the ability to order and to categorize, to have a scale of priorities is as useful and as valuable as the ability to inform. . . .

(5) Not the least of its values is its aid in acquiring a mastery of language. The mastery of language, however, must have as its prime objective, lucidity

of expression. . . . Waffle is more immediately apparent on paper. . . . To say what one means in no more than ten pages, or three-quarters of an hour, like hanging should concentrate the mind wonderfully. . . .

(6) Its development of personal qualities. To have strong views on a subject, matched perhaps by even stronger feelings, yet be forced to submit to the discipline of logic, dispassionate argument, utilisation of evidence, selection of facts, evaluation of opinions, is to throw into graphic relief the age old contest between one's heart and one's head. . . . It is, indeed, a valuable lesson to be required to substitute 'it may be argued' for 'I think'; 'one can therefore adduce' for 'I have proved'; 'one might aver' for 'I suggest'. . . .

(7) Its training in advocacy . . . it should act as an introduction to stimulate discussion and argument. . . . The essay allows both intellectual structure and varied arrangement, coherence without rigidity, shape without pattern. Narration is very often a constituent of an essay, just as history is a form of narration, if the essay allows digression it only reflects the variety of the historical process which cannot usually be tied down to one major theme.

(8) Above all history itself, by its nature, is essentially man's reflection on his past and the essay is an exercise in reflection. . . .

(9) Finally, the essay has, of course, an entirely utilitarian function; it provides a corpus of material for revision. Equally important it can provide a record of a student's intellectual growth and development. It is no doubt salutary but also encouraging; for it surely demonstrates to anyone looking back who wonders how they could have written such rubbish only eighteen months previously, that in the constant writing of essays lies the exercise of mental abilities that imperceptibly but nonetheless surely, grow stronger day by day.

So What can go Wrong?

Ralph Bennett wrote that:

> excellence in historical writing consists of simple and solid virtues, not of facile tricks and gaudy gadgets. . . . The candidate's chief protection . . . is his common sense. . . . "Answer the question." This is still the best single warning to keep in mind; let common sense tell you that "This is not an answer to the question set" must condemn even the finest essay for the good reason that it is hard to credit irrelevance (whether accidental, or apparently deliberate) with intellectual distinction.
>
> (R. Bennett (ed.), *First Class Answers in History*, Weidenfeld & Nicolson, 1974, pp. 2, 5, 123.)

Hugh Brogan was more insistent: 'Please, please, *please* read the question, and then answer *it*, and not some other.'

Arthur Marwick offered these thoughts:

> To answer the question you will need to analyse your material, not just present straight narrative or description. In writing essays students are often tempted to narrate for nine-tenths of the space at their disposal, then try to make up for this with a solid chunk of analysis at the end. This is a lazy and unsatisfactory way of writing an essay. When you are writing an essay, you should show that you are *thinking all the time*, not simply setting down information. You must . . . be selective in the material you include, making sure it is relevant to the question you have been asked. . . . Essentially the secret . . . is to try to break the question asked, or your thoughts about it, or (in the case of a history essay) the *relevant* material which you have gathered for the topic, down into meaningful single ideas or headings.
>
> (Open University, *Introduction to History* A 101, 3–5, p. 118, 1977)

In a report issued in 1981 the Oxford Delegacy of Local Examinations listed relevance as the 'absolutely crucial' criterion whose 'importance can hardly be over-emphasised. More candidates are unsuccessful through failure to answer the actual question set than for any other single reason.' The Delegacy also listed six types of irrelevance:

(a) simple disregard of the question asked;
(b) twisting the question to fit a prepared essay or line of argument or set of memorised quotations;
(c) partial irrelevance;
(d) 'saturation bombing', i.e. writing all one knows on a topic;
(e) superfluous narrative;
(f) partial or total misunderstanding of the question.

(It may be of interest that the Delegacy's 'major criteria of assessment' were 'relevance, argument and discussion, factual knowledge, organisation and presentation'.)

Planning the Essay

After reading and understanding the question, planning is the next priority. Ronald Hyam (in R. Bennett (ed.) *First Class Answers in History*, p. 138) identified four main types of plan:

(i) the *citadel* – one main point is massively buttressed into a central position by all supporting evidence with subsidiary defences laid out more superficially;
(ii) the *caravan* – like a wagon-train, this is a succession of more evenly weighted components;
(iii) the *comparative* – this integrates different characteristic aspects of countries and peoples compared at every step, not two largely unrelated halves;

(iv) the *critique* – this deals in historiography rather than history, and is unlikely to be used at 'A' level.

By now how to produce essays and what can go wrong should be taking shape in your mind; the Sackville Crowe exercise identified several aspects of historical writing without having a specific question to work from. How does this work in practice?

Example I. James II and the Revolution Settlement

'James II's policy was far more revolutionary than was the Revolution Settlement of 1688–89.' How far do you agree? (London Board)

Key words or phrases are 'policy' (was there a policy?), 'far more revolutionary than' (perhaps implying that James II's policies or the Glorious Revolution *were* to some degree revolutionary) and 'how far' (requiring a quantitative statement of extent). Next, we have to organise material and arrange ideas. Would a 'caravan' approach be suitable?

(A) (1) The early career of James, Duke of York, to 1685.
     (2) James's strengths and weaknesses as King.
     (3) The events of 1685–8: Monmouth's Rebellion;
                                 Roman Catholics in office;
                                 Seven Bishops.
     (4) The Glorious Revolution: the events of November–December 1688.
     (5) The Declaration of Rights.
     (6) The Toleration Act.
     (7) Conclusion.

Although this plan reveals that the writer may know the sequence of events in late-seventeenth-century England, there is little evidence that the *question* has been perceived. 'Good marks', the Oxford Delegacy informed, 'are awarded not so much for the sheer extent of a candidate's factual knowledge as for the selective use made of it. . . . The most common weakness of candidates lies in their failure to perceive which facts are relevant to the question.' Might, then, a more suitable plan be based on the 'comparative' model, taking each aspect in turn?

(B) *Introduction*: the background to the reign of James II;
     anti-popery in later Stuart England;
     standing army (compare Louis XIV);
     the favourable Parliament of 1685;
     the memory of 1649 – 'the hinge on which the century swung' and 1660;
     the desire of the gentry for stability *on their terms*;
     good lordship.

Kingship: James II's exalted view of kingship – had he learned the wrong lessons from Charles I and Charles II? – his bigotry;
A Roman Catholic Succession from Summer 1688?
The Monarch's Powers after 1689.
Parliament and the political nation: Loyalty up to a point;
R.C.s and Dissenters to replace C. of E. as J.P.s for example – lower social strata to rule Anglican superiors – fear of *social* revolution?
Borough charters (*Quo Warranto*);
Efforts to pack a new Parliament
Compare the above with the Declaration (Act) of Rights: No R.C. monarch, no High Commission; no army without parliamentary approval. Was this 'revolutionary' or retrospective legislation – Redress not Reform? But Parliament 'chose' the monarch and the Succession!
Finance: Compare James's financial base with that of Revolution Finance – taxes, national debt, the Bank of England, the 'monied interest', the Civil List. Some of these *after* 1689 so stress the limitation of the question; was the war against France the most important feature leading to revolutions in many aspects of government?
Law: Seven Bishops; Suspending Power; manipulation of the Judges and the magistrates. Compare with the Bill of Rights on the suspending power and illegal prosecutions, and on the status of Judges.
Religion: Catholicising policy *perceived* even if James had no coherent policy in fact;
James sought equality for co-religionists, but how to achieve this? And would this lead to supremacy and the eradication of Protestantism – look across the Channel at Louis XIV and the Huguenots, 1685;
R.C.s given a hierarchy and diocesan structure, public places of worship and education (Magdalen College, Oxford; Sidney Sussex College, Cambridge, for example);
Toleration Act – no comprehension but 'an unprecedented statutory security' (Langford) for dissenters, if not for R.C.s who had to wait until 1829. Did this lead to a tolerant, pluralist society in the eighteenth century? Was this revolutionary compared with James's ideas?
Foreign Affairs: James's policies seen to be very pro-French; William very anti-French – King William's War and the Marlborough Wars. Rise of British greatness?
The Armed Forces and Parliament; the size and prowess of British armies after 1689 (or should it be after 1702?)

A *Policy*: James guilty of self-deception – hoped for thousands of conversions;

James's foolishness and speed;

What would James have done but for 1688?

A *Revolution?* Role of William to protect wife's inheritance and defend powers of monarchy, which he feared would be lost if he did not act to lead *and* control the revolution, which would take place with or without him. 'For the British Constitution the years [1689–1701] were as formative as the Glorious Revolution itself.' (J. Carter) – especially 1694 Triennial Act; 1701 Act of Settlement; and the role of War;

Impact in Ireland (1690: Boyne) and Scotland (1689: Killiecrankie and Dunkeld): Three Kingdoms;

Were English kings – Charles I, James II or William III – more revolutionary than their subjects?

Examples should be used to support a point: in Lancashire, 67 J.P.s were in the last commission of Charles II's reign, but of these only four were in the last commission of his brother four years later! Or to support the 'revolution in finance' one could mention the 2,000 employed in the Excise by 1708. Similarly, a well-chosen quotation should succinctly express a point of view and not be chosen just because the historian is a well-known writer on the period.

This plan was too detailed for most purposes, especially for a forty-five minute examination essay, but its aim was to present a different structure from the 'caravan'. Ronald Hyam thought that 'the structural shape ideally should be clear enough to speak for itself'. He added that 'a building cannot be put up without scaffolding, but when it is finished, the scaffolding is removed. The cruder sign-posts of the plan should be eliminated.' So with this plan.

The following two paragraphs illustrate the plan in action; they are an Introduction and a paragraph on the revolutionary nature of the Settlement:

(1) No Stuart king came to the throne with as few problems as James II in 1685. The royalist reaction to the Popish Plot and Exclusion Crisis, including the rout of Charles II's opponents and the successful remodelling of the charters of corporate boroughs, ensured a peaceful and popular succession. James was an experienced military and naval commander and had been an active viceroy for his brother in Scotland. His first marriage had been happy and fruitful – two protestant daughters – and, in contrast to his brother, James had only one mistress, Arabella Churchill. His first Parliament was warm and generous, enabling the King to increase his standing army. The formidable memory of 1649 – 'the hinge on which the century swung' (J. P. Kenyon) – and the desire of the political nation for stability should have acted in James's favour. But two clouds drifted across the sun: the gentry and nobility were only prepared to accept stability on *their* terms, and James had been an avowed Roman Catholic since 1673 with a bigoted Italian for his second wife. The paranoia of the Popish Plot, only the

most recent of 130 years of anti-catholic propaganda, showed the perils of tolerating popery, but would James heed the warnings? Did he believe that it had been his father's weakness that had undone the Royalist cause in the 1640s, and that the lesson to be learned was to be strong and unyielding? Had he learned the wrong lessons from recent history?

(2) It would appear that the effects of the Revolution, or its aftermath, were more revolutionary than the so-called Glorious Revolution itself. Was there then any sense in which 1688–9 was revolutionary? William felt it necessary to intervene to protect his inheritance and defend the powers of monarchy which he feared would be lost if he did not act to lead and control the revolution, which would take place with or without him. For William or Mary to have been nominated *in absentia* by the Lords and Commons or 'the people of England' would have been more revolutionary; as it was, William was able to control the events of 1688–9 and act decisively to preserve the royal prerogative. In some ways he may have prevented a greater revolution. Geoffrey Holmes once referred to 1688 as the 'unnecessary revolution'; so it may have been in England, but what about Scotland and Ireland? The impact there lasted longer with battles at Killiecrankie and Dunkeld in Scotland in 1689 and at the Boyne in Ireland the following year. The latter ensured a Protestant ascendancy until the early twentieth century, and may be considered one of the more revolutionary aspects of the Revolution Settlement.

Example II. The Rise of Fascism

The second essay question is from twentieth-century Europe:
Analyse the factors which promoted the growth of Fascism in Italy in the immediate post-war years. (Northern Universities Joint Matriculation Board)
As in the previous example, first thoughts may be towards a 'caravan'-style plan. Here are some points on the topic to guide you:

Recent unification of Italy in the mid nineteenth century; the problems of this, especially the gulf between north and south, industrial and agrarian. (See *Christ Stopped at Eboli*, Carlo Levi.)

Perceptions of Fascism: how much was revealed about the true nature of the movement before 1922?

Mythology and propaganda: the myth of 'the march on Rome' and the cult of Mussolini.

The impact of the First World War and the 'lost peace' – *Italia irredenta*.

The spectre of Communism.

D'Annunzio and Futurism – the mood of 1918–22.

Politics: the procession of ministries and the shallow roots of democracy.

The War, Inflation and the Middle Classes.

Such ideas as these should be buzzing around in your mind while the plan is being formulated. What, one may ask, is a factor? Jonathan Steinberg denied ever having seen an historical factor. Does it mean something impersonal or beyond human control? It is equally a truism, perhaps, to assert that 'people cause events'. Yet there are circumstances in which the mood of the time – the

Zeitgeist – exerts an influence on people. Fascism may have been one such mood, enabling individuals to sink themselves and their problems into a mass movement, 'anchored in responsibility in a party' as M. Buber put it.

Now see if you can plan this essay using the ideas mentioned above and some reading of your own. If your period of history falls outside the two examples chosen in this chapter do not worry. It is not possible to include an example from every period, and the lessons that can be drawn from the examples here may be transferred to essays within your period. Once your mind has become attuned to the processes by which essays are planned and written, then the concepts may be applied across the whole spectrum of history with very few modifications.

Examination Essays

The final section of this chapter looks at essays written in examination conditions in forty-five minutes, particularly at two examples from the early seventeenth century. This enables us to put the lessons learned into practice again, and to examine critically how other young historians faced the problems.

Example III. Charles I and the 1630s

Had Charles I's subjects any good reason to be dissatisfied with his government in the 1630s?

This question concerns the period known sometimes as the 'Personal Rule' or even as the 'eleven years' tyranny'; it was the decade during which Charles I did not summon Parliament. Key aspects of the question might be:

Who were his 'subjects'? The political nation – gentry and nobility – or the whole population?

'Any good reason' might suggest in the minds of contemporaries, or what *we* might suppose to be good reasons to a seventeenth–century Englishman, including deep feelings on anti-popery, for example. This may depend on the definition of 'subjects'.

'Dissatisfied' could take several forms, from informal discussion by the gentry at quarter sessions through non-payment of taxes to civil disobedience and riot. Can the 1630s be judged by the action taken in the early 1640s by the Long Parliament, and how far into that decade can retrospective action be taken as a judgement on the 1630s? Does 'government' extend to Scotland, a country of which King Charles was undeniably sovereign, but which was a *foreign* country to many Englishmen?

All these aspects are quite apart from the grievances themselves which need to be investigated.

The first essay is given in full with comments given opposite. Do you agree with the comments? Are there additional remarks that you would make?

Text	Comment
It has to be borne in mind when discussing this question that we have the advantage of hindsight. It may be possible to look back now and claim, justifiably, that Charles I had no intention of establishing either absolutism or Catholicism in England, but the people of England in the 1630s could only see the outward face of Charles' policy, not the motives behind it. What is more, in citing the views of Charles I's subjects we have to disregard the illiterate, disregarded 90% of the population whose views we do not know.	Taking for granted that what follows is true: is it? *No* intention? Who were the 'people'? A good point, clumsily expressed.
Charles' government in the 1630's differed from earlier reigns in that he ruled between 1629 and 1640 without calling a parliament. Dissolving parliament in 1629 after an angry session he undertook to prove that he could rule alone. At no stage did he claim to rule absolutely and there is little question that once he had ordered his state to his own satisfaction he would recall parliament. The dissatisfaction with the 'personal rule' was not constitutional, it was only after 1638, and the outbreak of the Bishops' Wars that it began to be felt that Charles should call a parliament to vote money.	Elizabeth I and James I had long periods without Parliament. 'Alone'? Good point 'Felt' by whom? And for any other reasons?
During the personal rule Charles had to break certain traditions in order to survive without a parliament. Financially he was compelled to demand unparliamentary taxation and to enforce certain dues, such as forest fines and knighthood fines which his predecessors neglected. Obviously the brunt of such dues fell on the gentry and nobility who although most capable of paying had previously been largely immune from taxation as a result of their power within the local communities. The introduction of a new rate, Ship money greatly disrupted these communities as the crown appointed commissioners and there was confusion as to who was in charge. Athough Hampden argued against Ship Money on constitutional grounds, it was largely paid until 1638 and the demand for money to fight the Scots. Financially Charles spread the demand for money more evenly and it was this which led to the grievance expressed in the Grand Remonstrance in 1641.	Brief but useful on 'traditions'. 'Compelled'? Use of examples. Should one use 'obviously'? Small point: use commas for clarity. Were the gentry 'immune' as in France? Stress inequality of taxation. Was Ship Money 'new'? Valid point but again clumsily handled. Brief on the nature and implications of the Hampden Case. True.
It was people as much as policies which worried the English. Charles' chief minister in Ireland, Strafford, exerted a powerful hand over all sections of the Irish community and, being of low birth himself took apparent delight in bringing down members of the nobility. In particular he hounded the Earl of Cork	Yes; make the point of the English fear of the Irish, and of Ireland being a training-ground before England. Good sentence on Cork!

mercilessly. This instilled fear into the souls of nobles in England who dreaded his return home. This is apparent in the speed with which writs were drawn up against him as soon as the House of Commons met in 1640. Yet he frightened the ordinary people too by threatening the hierarchy of social order. If he could bring down great men, what would he do to lesser men?

> A good point on the lower orders.
> Rhetorical questions reasonable, if explained.

It was perhaps Charles' religious policy as practised by Laud and Strafford which terrified the English most. England was traditionally anti-Catholic, a reaction to Smithfield and Mary's persecution of protestants and a fond memory of Elizabeths' reign. Under Laud a policy of Arminianism or apparent arminianism (in ceremony but not in doctrine) was introduced into English churches. Laud believed in 'the beauty of Holiness' and although he wrote one of the best defences of the Church of England, men saw only the trappings of popery. Laud also introduced a vigorous programme of reform including metropolitical visitation and fines for badly educated clerics which antagonised vested interests. Like Wolsely before him Laud suffered for his 'mean extraction', the high born resented his power. The threat of Catholicism was not merely religious but also political. The Long Parliament of November 1640 was to be referred to as 'A squire's protest against sacerdotal politics'. Asked what Arminians held, it was once replied 'all the best deaneries and bishoprics in the land'. In other words, it was feared that Catholicism was beginning to affect Charles' government. Looking at it from a contemporary's point of view Charles himself was surrounded by papists for his wife was a Catholic as were her friends and entourage.

> Good points on anti-popery.
>
> Stress on ceremonies: debate on this complex and confusing!
>
> *Perception* of Laud.
> Good phrase on popery – examples?
>
> Examples? Feoffees?
> Which 'vested interests'?
> *Wolsely*. An interesting comparison.
>
> Author of the quotation? But a good quote.
> Should this have come earlier?
> Is it an accurate quote?
>
> Note the structure of this sentence.
> What does this mean?

During Charles' reign government became stricter. The law courts were tightened up on and punishments became harsher. Charles and his ministers sought to help the poor in a period of adverse harvests and the book of orders published in 1631 laid down provisions to do so – what is more they were enforced until 1638.

> Too short on legal examples. Who were his other ministers?
> Useful, but we need examples.
> e.g. enclosure, corn-engrossing.

The personal rule was not, until the outbreak of war in '38, a time of disruption. People apparently accepted rule without parliament. When trouble in the Celtic fringe led Charles to demand extra taxation, however, people began to recognise other grievances and, eventually began to call for a parliament. Nevertheless there was much in the policies of Charles I which, without knowledge of his intentions could frighten people. Catholicism was a major terror and it has to be admitted that the new prayer book

> True. 1638 in full.
>
> Scottish prayer book? See below. Generalisation of 'people'.
>
> Good on perception.

introduced into Scotland in 1638 makes defence of Lauds policy more difficult. With the example of France on the continent and their enemy Spain fear of absolutism was understandable. They did not know that without army or bureaucracy Charles could never have fought a war alone. Hence, although with hindsight the Englishmen of the 1630's had nothing to fear, they were not unreasonable to question their monarch's intentions during the 'personal rule'.

Mention the Thirty Years' War. *Whose* enemy? What was English foreign policy in 1630s? A Spanish army in 1640?
Perception again.
'Nothing to fear'?

What were Charles's aims? Note his deviousness, and the distrust he had created by 1640. Was he fit to govern?

Discuss the merits of this essay in general, as well as analysing the particular criticisms. Did it answer the question, was it sufficiently broad and deep? Were there enough examples?

The second example illustrates the perils of historiography: only the first two paragraphs are given here, without comment.

Recent opinion of historians of the seventeenth century has looked far greater at the period of the Personal Rule, 1629–1640 to find the explanations for the outbreak of Civil War in 1642. Members of this 'Revisionist School' such as Mr. K. Sharpe and Mr. C. Russel have propounded their beliefs that it was in these years that the foundations for the Civil War were laid, the grievances against Charles government coming more from his mis-management of the system of government than of long-term inherent faults which made this civil war an inevitable result of the changes in views and economic power. Whichever theory is believed to be the most credible, both place great emphasis on the 1630s, as the key years which either sparked off or began the Civil War.

The years 1640–2 saw the airing of these grievances and a great deal towards their settlement by the 'Short and Long Parliaments'. Thus it is more convenient to use the things which they stated as their grievances rather than to speculate as to what these were. For many, especially Oliver Cromwell, it was religion that was the ultimate deciding force in turning him against the crown, as it was also for John Pym. In fact John Morrill believed that the Civil War was 'the last and greatest of Europe's wars of religion'. Religion was the area in which there was greatest opposition to the crown, rather than constitutional or economic. For example in the time when the parliamentary system was greatly distorted by the exclusion of the Bishops, there were four times as many pamphlets concerning the now unobtrusive canons issued beforehand, than what we now see to be the great constitutional issue of excluding Bishops from the Lords. It is perhaps a sign of the decline in our contemporary opinion of the importance of religion that we do not give it enough emphasis in this time.

There are some nuggets here, but they are very well hidden among a plethora of irrelevance and some confusion and obscurity: consider the plight of the examiner!

Example IV. Anti-Popery

The last exercise in this chapter is to assess an essay without guidance. Remember that we are looking for relevance; analysis; depth; accuracy of information and language; style; and also a sense of history, a feeling of excitement which makes us fascinated in what we are reading. Does this essay have any of these points to a large extent?

'Gunpowder, Treason and Plot.' Why did early seventeenth-century Englishmen tend to see the Roman Catholics in this way?

By the beginning of the seventeenth-century anti-Catholicism was a firmly established feature of England. The early C17th Englishmen tended to see Catholics in terms of 'Gunpowder, treason and plot'. It may be that these anti-catholic feelings had the same psychological origins as the anti-Jewish or anti-Communist feelings during the twentieth century. These groups were used as a scape-goat for the problems of society and during the sixteenth and seventeenth century, wherever problems occurred the Catholics were often blamed for it.

During James I reign the Catholics became associated with 'Gunpowder, treason and plot', yet anti-Catholic feeling went a great deal further back than this. The hatred of Catholics derived from a distorted version of history, and Protestants felt that history repeated itself in cyclical patterns. Thus events in the past showing Catholics to be an evil sect, were felt to show that Catholics could not be trusted.

The Protestant looked back into the C16th and found a great deal of evidence to show that the Catholics were intent on the extermination of the Protestants using unscrupulous and bloody means. One of the memories most vividly kept alive was the burning of Protestants for heresy, during Mary I time. There was a great deal of propaganda which emphasised the murders of the Protestants during this time and one book was found widely in ealy C17th Englishmens houses. This was Foxes 'Book of Matyrs' which illustrated in horrific detail the Catholic burnings of Protestants. Thus Mary became a most unpopular Queen particuraly as she insisted on marrying the Catholic Spanish King, Phillip, and seemingly directing England towards the Pope. Her successor Elizabeth I was far more popular and the English victory over the Spanish Armada was felt to show that God had lost faith in the Catholics.

Looking back at foreign history, Protestants also felt that there was evidence of Catholic despotism, for example, the Alva Council of the blood in the Netherlands, the Marian burnings and the St Bartholomews day massacre in 1672. Protestants felt that the Catholic revival in France might also threaten England and ruin the English Protestant Church.

Thus by the beginning of the seventeenth century a very black and white image had grown up. Protestants contrasted the purity of their church with the supposed corruption of the Catholic church. The extent of this hatred can be seen quite clearly as the Pope was known to Protestants as anti-Christ. Within England during this period xenophobia was strong particurly against Spain. The Protestants connected the Catholics with the Jesuits and in turn Spain. Thus the Catholics were thought to be on the side of foreign intevention and absolute monarchy, wheras the Protestants were on the side of the government and the rule of law. By the C17th Catholicism had become a treasonable element subject to a battery of penal laws which were designed to inhibit worship, ruin finances, arrest conversion and ruin the priesthood. Catholics therefore were at a great disadvantage within society.

When James I came to the throne, the Catholics felt they had a much greater chance as James was prepared to give the Catholics a certain amount of toleration. However James alternated between being harsh upon the Catholics and being tolerant towards them. Therefore the Catholics became very disillusioned, and the Protestants began to feel that they could not trust James. The Catholics out of desperation turned to extreme measures towards James, and many plots grew up to kidnap or kill James and his ministers and convert England to a Catholic country. These plots includes the main, Bye and Watson plot all of which failed for the Catholics and were used as propaganda to increase hatred towards the Catholics. These plots were looked upon as evidence that the Catholics were evil and the Protestants felt that their religion was threatened and felt somewhat intimadated by the Catholics. In February 1605 James inaugurated a purge against recusants, yet this failed to eliminate the most famous plot of all against James. This was the Gunpowder plot of 1605, which was thought to be a Catholic plot led by Guy Fawkes to blow up both the Houses of Parliament. The plot was discovered and the plotters arrested and killed. Although a great deal of speculation surrounds the plot, as to whether it was actually a Catholic plot or a set-up by the government, the Protestants believed firmly at the time that it was a Catholic plot. This provided them with irrefutable confirmation of their prejudices and suspicions and anti-Catholicism was reinforced. Although James only imposed another two penal laws against the Catholics the Gun-powder plot ruined the position of Catholics still further and they became connected with 'Gunpowder, treason and plot'.

The accusations that the Protestants brought against the Catholics were in the majority of cases most unfair. Most Catholics simply wished to practise their religion in peace, yet events which showed Catholic despotism in the sixteenth century was still being thrown into the face of seventeenth-century Catholics. The hatred towards Catholics had gradually been built up over the years and reached a climax during the seventeenth century. James I was an inteligent man and realised that the Catholics posed no real threat to the kingdom, yet it was clear that a much greater force than himself would be needed to eliminate the deep-rooted bigotry of Englishmen, whose narrow-mindedness meant that the Catholics were seen in terms of 'Gunpowder, treason and Plot'.

(Written by a Lower Sixth pupil in an examination four months after the start of the course. The essay was timed for about 45 minutes.)

Types of Examination Question

In a very useful booklet, L. G. Brandon (*History: A Guide to Advanced Study*, Edward Arnold 1976) stated that 'the examiner assumes that candidates have brought with them a useful stock of historical evidence. From that stock he wants them to select material which has a clear bearing upon problems concerning:

the aims of individuals or groups;
achievements;
the significance of the achievements;
the causes and results of the actions of individuals or groups;
general assessments of the character or achievements of one person with those of another;
comparison of the causes or results of one set of events with those of another set;
the nature of important 'movements' and trends;
particular opinions, written by historians, upon any of these matters;

the process by which historians arrive at their knowledge and their judgments.'

Brandon also listed ten types of questions according to one or more 'guide words'. These are reproduced here with a few additional features:

(i) The most common guide words are very general – *'Discuss'*, *'Consider'*, *'Comment upon'*. Candidates are free to express their own opinions and to make any observations which are appropriate to the main wording of the question. These general instructions may be assumed, normally, to indicate any of the operations which are discussed later. But if the topic is presented in the form of a quotation, it must be assumed that the passage has been chosen with the specific purpose of provoking a discussion upon each of its parts. . . . It asks for the candidate's opinions, and he alone knows what they are. But he must show his ability by supporting them with good evidence and sound argument.

(ii) *'Explain'* is rather more definite. It means 'show that you have understood why things were as they were or happened as they did'. 'Explain the main differences between the teachings of Luther and the teachings of Calvin' sets a difficult task, because it involves not only knowing what the doctrines were but also understanding how each man came to assert his particular beliefs.

(iii) *'Examine'* strictly means 'test' or 'enquire into'. . . .

(iv) *'Assess'*, *'Estimate'*, *'To what extent?'*, *'How far?'* 'Assess' means 'to fix an amount' or 'to find the value of'. There is a clear indication that something is to be measured, even though the answer cannot be expressed in numbers. The other three terms give the same guidance. The topic to be considered concerns achievements, influences or other matters which can vary widely in importance or amount. The candidate is asked to weigh up his evidence and to reach a conclusion which shows the significance of certain aspects of the topic. . . .

(v) *'Illustrate and account for'*, *'Trace and account for'*. These guide words are dangerous, because they ask for a descriptive statement, to be followed by a discussion of causes. There is a temptation for candidates to give a simple narrative account, and to ignore the second part of the question. . . .

(vi) *'What is the significance of?'* This invites consideration of the important consequences of a man's political, economic or artistic work. It suggests the questions: 'What did he do? What was its value?', 'How has the value been judged?', 'Who benefited from it?'. It may also be used to ask for the results of actions and events, over a short or long period of time. . . . Thus 'significance' includes not only results, but also any inferences which can be made from the evidence which is studied.

(vii) *'What were the principles underlying . . .?'*

(viii) *'Compare and contrast'* (the foreign policies of Castlereagh and Canning). The instruction is clear enough. The important matter is to decide how the answer is to be arranged: whether to make the comparison step by step, or whether to deal first with Castlereagh and then with Canning, indicating the similarities and differences in some concluding paragraphs. The first method is usually better, but the one thing to avoid is a mixture of the two patterns.

(ix) '*What were the problems facing*' (Elizabeth I on her accession?) This demands careful thinking about the problems as they would be understood at the time, not as we have come to think about them since.

(x) '*What considerations influenced*' (Joseph Chamberlain's reaction to the Jameson raid?) This means: 'Why did he act as he did after the raid?' As a question about thoughts and motives it is very difficult to answer with assurance.

An essay type that has developed since Brandon wrote is the imaginative:

(1) Imagine that you are Louis XIV writing your memoirs at the end of your reign. How would you justify your handling of foreign affairs since about 1680?
(2) Write a description of social and political life in the United Provinces as it might have appeared to a French visitor in the middle of the seventeenth century.
(3) Write an editorial which might have appeared during the 1874 election assessing Gladstone's achievements as Prime Minister.

The historian cannot be transported back in time, so his imagination must be tempered by the knowledge of what is known and what might have transpired. He is not writing historical fiction (see Tranter's novel on James I in Chapter 1) and must convince the reader that his grasp of the events and their significance is at least equal to that of the contemporary, who lacked hindsight. The writer should also show that he understands the viewpoint and character of the contemporary whom he represents. This is not easy, and answers could be vague or unconvincing. It is hard to envisage a very good answer on (1) which did not reveal evidence of having read St Simon, or at least a good modern biography of Louis XIV. Imagination must start with the evidence, often returning to it with the ability to see it in a new light. The actions and beliefs of predecessors must be seen as rational within their frame of reference. 'We are no smarter than our ancestors' was one of Jonathan Steinberg's 'Laws of History', and it would be ridiculous to decry Louis XIV as a 'fool' for accepting the Spanish throne on behalf of his grandson in 1700.

These 'imaginative' or 'empathetic' questions are now more common in examinations, but should be treated with respect.

3 Primary Evidence – An Introduction

'documents are liars. No man ever yet tried to write down the entire truth of any action in which he was engaged'

If it is ever possible to find out 'the truth' about the past – and most historians would agree with T. E. Lawrence's assertion – then the key to this process lies in the use of evidence. Although 'sources' are sometimes regarded as exclusively written or printed material we have used the term interchangeably with 'evidence'. It may be incomplete, biased, partial: but it is the basic raw material for even the simplest attempts at historical reconstruction. This chapter will place primary evidence within the broad framework of historical analysis and the following three chapters will examine both it and secondary evidence in more detail.

Primary evidence suffers from certain major limitations. Out of all the actions and interactions that make up the human past only a minute part of that past has been written down and will have survived. Before historians begin their work on evidence it has already been filtered. It has been filtered by limited recording since only a small proportion of past happenings will have been committed to some communicable form. It has been filtered by limited observation; not everything seen will have been observed and consciously held in the individual's memory and recorded later. Finally there has been limited survival of evidence; some is lost or destroyed or has decayed with age. The evidence we have is already incomplete. 'The truth' in an absolute sense is just not available. Historians cannot verify, they can only examine, empathise and attempt to explain. All we can say is that there is evidence that this person once existed or that event took place and that given the available evidence this is a possible, tenable explanation of what motivated the individual or caused the event.

Types of Evidence

There are two main types of evidence used by historians. *Primary* sources were produced during the period that the historian is studying. They are documents or artefacts produced by eyewitnesses, participants in or commentators on the events the historian is attempting to reconstruct and explain. Without them history as a discipline could not exist. *Secondary* sources are the products of historians writing using primary sources. They reconstruct, interpret and provide a coherent and plausible account of what happened in the past, why and how. But the distinction between primary and secondary sources is not always well defined. In 1587 John Knox published *A History of the Reformation in Scotland*. Primary or secondary? Despite being a coherent, if personal, history of religious change it is primary because of the evidence of those changes which it contains. Macaulay's multi-volume *History of England*, published between 1848 and 1861, is a secondary source for the history of late seventeenth-century Britain but a primary source if the historian is examining nineteenth-century historical method. Of two biographies of Adolf Hitler, one by Konrad Heiden published in 1936 and a second by Alan Bullock published in 1953, the former is primary, the latter secondary. Look at the following pieces of evidence – some on Louis XIV and others on Britain in the 1930s. Which are primary and which secondary?

(1) J. B. Bossuet, *Politique tirée des propres paroles de l'Ecriture Sainte*, written *c.* 1670 (first published 1709)
(2) M. de Voltaire, *Le Siècle de Louis XIV* (first published 1751)
(3) *Historical Memoirs of the Duc de Saint-Simon* (Hamish Hamilton, 1958)
(4) J. B. Wolf, *Louis XIV: A Profile* (Macmillan, 1972)
(5) P. Erlanger, *Louis XIV* (Weidenfeld and Nicolson, 1970)
(6) *The Private Life of the Marshal Duke of Richelieu*, translated by F. S. Flint (1958)
(7) *Lettres, instructions et mémoires de Colbert*, ed. by P. Clement (Paris, 1867)
(8) *Le Clerc Le Triomphe de la Foy* (1686), translated in J. B. Wolf *Louis XIV* (1968)
(9) *Lettres de Louis XIV*, ed. P. Gaxotte (Paris, 1930)
(10) F. Charpentier, *Concerning the Establishment of a French Company for the Commerce of the East Indies* (1664)
(11) J. Stevenson, *British Society 1914–45* (Penguin edn, 1984)
(12) G. D. H. Cole and M. I. Cole, *The Condition of Britain* (Gollancz, 1937)
(13) H. Tout, *The Standard of Living in Bristol* (Bristol University Press, 1938)
(14) G. Orwell, *The Road to Wigan Pier* (Penguin edn, 1972)
(15) J. B. Priestley, *English Journey* (Heinemann, 1934)
(16) G. C. M. M'Gonigle and J. Kirby, *Poverty and Public Health* (Gollancz, 1937)
(17) M. Muggeridge, *The Thirties* (1940)
(18) J. Symons, *The Thirties: A Dream Revolved* (1960)
(19) H. Forrester, *Twopence to Cross the Mersey* (1974)
(20) B. L. Coombes, *These Poor Hands* (1939)

There are many different types of primary evidence. Look at the list of sources below and suggest ways of grouping them.

Acreage returns
Alehouses
Apprenticeships
Bishops' records
Borough records
British Transport Authority
    records
Buses
Canals
Censuses
Charity Commission
    Reports
Churchwardens' accounts
Deeds
Directories
Domesday Book
Ecclesiastical Commissioners'
    records
Enclosure awards
Field names
Films
Freemen's rolls
Gild records
Grave stones
Hedges
House of Lords
    records
Hundred Rolls
Inquisitions post
    mortem
Land taxes
Leases
Letters
Literary sources
Manorial records
Memoirs
Monasteries
Music Halls
Newspapers
Oral evidence
Parish registers

Acts of Parliament
Almshouses
Banks
Blue books
Bridges
Buildings

Business records
Castles
Chantry certificates
Charters

Date stones
Diaries
Dissenters' certificates
Drama
Ecclesiastical records

Estate records
Fire insurance records
Folk songs
Friaries
Glebe terriers
Hearth tax assessments
Hospitals
Housing

Improvement Commissions
Inventories

Lay subsidies
Legends
Legislation
Local government reports
Maps
Militia papers
Muster rolls
Myths
Novels
O. S. Maps
Poll books

Photographs
Poetry
Poll tax
Posters
Protestation Returns
Quarter Sessions records
Radio broadcasts
Railway records
Recusancy papers
Roads
Sewer Commission records
Surrey Iron railway
Tithe records
Town defences
Trams

Vestry minutes
Water Company
  records
Workhouses

Place names
Portraits
Poor Law records
Prints
Pubs
Queen Anne's Bounty
Radios
Rate books
Registration certificates
School Board Records
Spas
Tape recordings

Town names
Turnpike Trust
  records
Visitation records

Wills

The largest body of evidence is made up of materials that are written, either in manuscript or in some printed form. There are other categories and it is convenient to distinguish written, visual and oral types of evidence. Look at these two pieces of evidence.

(1) A Venetian view of Henry VIII

His Majesty is the handsomest potentate I ever set eyes on; above the usual height, with an extremely fine calf to his leg; his complexion fair and bright, with auburn hair combed straight and short in the French fashion, and a round face so beautiful that it would become a pretty woman. . . . He speaks French, English, Latin and a little Italian; plays well on the lute and harpsichord, sings from the book on sight, draws the bow with greater strength than any man in England, and jousts marvellously.
(*Letters and Papers, Foreign and Domestic, of the Reign of Henry VIII, 1509–47*, ed. Brewer, Gairdner and Brodie, 1862–1910, vol. ii, 395)

(2) A Holbein Portrait (Figure 3.1).

List five things it is possible to say about Henry VIII from each piece of evidence. What are the differences between the two lists?

The distinction between written and visual evidence is particularly important. Written evidence, such as a diplomatic paper or a letter or a newspaper report, tends to tell historians something *specific* about people and events. It was produced to communicate feelings, information, ideas, words. But visual evidence tells historians things of a more *general* nature about a

Figure 3.1

society and its culture. Although historians can use the Holbein portrait to obtain an impression of what Henry looked like it is far more valuable as a source for painting styles, the technology of sixteenth-century art, fashion and so on. We discover little from the portrait about Henry as a person. To find out what Henry could do or what he believed or feared then historians have to turn to the written accounts.

Evaluation of Primary Written Evidence

There are rules for using written, visual and oral sources, but since most of the raw material historians use is to be found in some sort of document we will concentrate on written evidence. Although there is an infinite variety of documents there are certain routine questions which need to be asked of them *all*. The French historian Marc Bloch wrote of the 'struggle with documents', the unravelling of the records of the past by historians. This is the process of 'internalising' the evidence. Historians have two aims. First they must determine whether the evidence is *authentic*. Then they must establish the *meaning* and *credibility* of its contents.

(1) Authenticity

Testing for authenticity is known as external criticism. This means establishing that the document is what it purports to be and that it is in its most accurate form. This is a major problem for medievalists, who have to deal with charters and other legal documents which may have been forged, either to replace lost originals or to claim lands or rights which had never been granted. The most famous is the eighth-century Donation of Constantine, shown in the fifteenth century to be a forgery, which supposedly gave temporal power over Italy to Pope Sylvester I and his successors. The recent case over the Hitler Diaries shows that there is still a market for forgeries.

To find out whether a document is genuine can be a complex process requiring many different skills. Extensive knowledge of the period in question is essential. Does the document fit in with what we know of the period? Can we trace the document back to the individual or institution that produced it? One of the problems with the authenticity of the Turin Shroud is a break in its chronology. Is it accurate? Before the invention of printing, documents were copied by hand with the inevitable discrepancies which increased as each copy was used as the basis for another. Can we find the original? Do the parchment, paper and ink and the language fit with the period? Carbon dating and chemical analysis can reveal the age of paper, parchment and ink. The Vinland Map was shown to be a forgery when chemical analysis of its ink showed man-made pigments unknown before this century.

(2) Interpretation

Once historians have established the authenticity of a document then comes the challenge of reading and interpreting its contents – the process of internal criticism. All documents have been produced by fallible and potentially dishonest human beings. Even an account written by a person of unimpeachable honesty can be biased and tell half-truths. What sort of questions should historians ask?

(i) What does the document *mean*? This may mean either translating the document from Greek, Latin or Arabic in the first instance or using someone else's translation. It means looking at the words used. What, for example, is meant by a 'serf' in documents in England and Russia? What was a 'forty-shilling freeholder' or a 'radical' in early nineteenth-century Britain? Language and the meaning of words change through time. George Kitson Clark gives 'enthusiasm' as an example in *The Critical Historian*. Dr Johnson's definition in 1755 was 'a vain belief in private revelation; a vain confidence of divine power or communication'. This is not the modern sense of the word. There is often a difference between the *literal* meaning of a document and its *real* meaning. Sometimes it is necessary to read between the lines to find out what was really meant. For example, several letters survive of 1830–2 from a Hertfordshire clergyman describing his part in putting down a riot near Luton. His account differs from reports in the *Northampton Mercury*. Why? His aim, stated in his last letter, was clerical preferment and so he probably exaggerated his role. Being unaware of this historians could easily take the literal meaning as truth whereas it is a personal view of the event.

(ii) What about the *author*? Is all primary evidence of equal value? The simple answer is no. Some sources are more credible and reliable than others. Evidence is often produced at some distance from the event it describes, so historians need to look closely at the relationship between author and event.

EVENT	PROBLEMS
Eyewitness – first-hand evidence	Was it produced immediately after? Was it produced afterwards with more thought? Have subsequent events influenced the account? How much of the event was seen?
Contemporary account – evidence once removed	What eyewitness accounts were used? How many years after the event? Motives for producing account?
Contemporary comment – evidence twice removed	Opinions based upon event? Bias? Prejudice?

How might the author's social or economic position have influenced the way the event was seen? For example, policemen saw the disturbances in London in 1848 differently from the Chartists. People who took part in the 'hunger-marches' in the 1930s saw things differently from the National Government.

(iii) Can historians *trust* what the author says? Is what is written *fair*? Diaz's account of human sacrifice in Aztec Mexico, the antipathy of some medieval chroniclers for William Rufus and King John, John Milton's distaste for the Anglican Church, Stalin's hatred for Trotsky, all reflect the prejudice that is a dominant human characteristic. The intentions and prejudices of authors affect the reliability of documents more than anything else. Authors generally have personal beliefs or convictions that influence their view of events. Is the author making a 'fair comment'? Or is there evidence of 'bias' – an often *unconscious* reflection of social, economic and political circumstances – or 'prejudice' – a *conscious*, often irrationally held belief frequently based on myths, misunderstandings and misinformation. Historians have to check not merely the bias of evidence but also their own.

Documents produced by governments or by governmental institutions have to be treated with great care. In the nineteenth century politicians' letters were frequently used as the basis for a memoir and were selected to give a favourable impression. Royal Commissions and Select Committees were often composed of people who had pronounced views on the particular issue. Evidence was selected which sustained their preconceived views and the conclusions they desired emerged. This is clearly the case with the Report of the Royal Commission on the Poor Laws published in 1834. Examples of good practice under the old Poor Laws were given far less prominence than instance of bad practice so that the general condemnation of the old system and its reform could be maintained.

(iv) In what ways was the evidence produced and for what purpose? Is it *private* or *public* evidence? Was it produced by a government or some other public organisation or institution either to record what happened or to put forward a case to a wider audience (e.g. *Hansard*, minutes of the Poor Law Commission, Royal Commissions) *or* was it produced privately by individuals for themselves or for close relatives or friends (e.g. diaries, private letters)?

Was it produced by some organisation or individual with *specific intentions* – to inform, to make a case, to impress, to justify past or subsequent actions – *or* was it produced *unintentionally* as part of the normal process of life? Documents provide not only intended evidence but also an 'unwitting testimony'. Some sources are valued for information that authors unwittingly conveyed while setting down what was purely incidental to their purposes. We can learn much about assumptions, attitudes, beliefs and prejudices from such unconscious testimony.

(v) The source must be placed in the proper *context*. The general framework of society, the economic, institutional and political structure and the nature of ideas all need to be considered since they do provide insight into the real meaning of the evidence. It would be very misleading for historians concerned with eighteenth-century British politics to approach the subject as though the nature of 'constitutional monarchy' or 'the cabinet' were unchanged. At the same time it is only through the examination and evaluation of primary evidence that historians can fully establish what the context is.

(vi) Is there *corroboration* or *confirmation*? One of the ways to establish the credibility of a particular piece of evidence is to find corroborating testimony.

It is possible to fill in the table below for each piece of evidence which historians use.

IS THE EVIDENCE	YES/NO	COMMENTS
Written		
Visual		
Oral		
Eyewitness		
Contemporary account		
Contemporary comment		
Private		
Public		
Intentional		
Unintentional		

Practical Use of Evidence: An Example

On 16th August 1819 a mass meeting took place in St Peter's Field, Manchester, in support of parliamentary reform. It ended with several people killed and many injured when the local yeomanry and some regular troops attempted to arrest Henry Hunt and other speakers. There were many different accounts of these events. Your task is to determine what actually happened on that fateful August day. The following points will help you to do this effectively:

(1) Examine each piece of evidence *in turn* using the techniques outlined above.
(2) Which pieces of evidence do you think are of most value to you in constructing your narrative? Why?
(3) Produce a chronology for each document of the event.
(4) Are there any discrepancies between the different pieces of evidence? Can you resolve them satisfactorily?
(5) Is it possible to adduce causation? In what ways?
(6) Produce your narrative. How do you want to present the information?
(7) Compare your account with those of other students. How can you account for any differences?
(8) Reassess your own account.

Source A: Contemporary Cartoon (Figure 3.2)

Figure 3.2

Source B: Samuel Bamford

On the cavalry drawing up they were received with a shout of goodwill, as I understood it. They shouted again, waving their sabres over their heads; and then, slackening rein, and striking spur into their steeds, they dashed forward and began cutting the people. 'Stand fast,' I said, 'they are riding upon us, stand fast.' And there was a general cry in our quarter of 'Stand fast'. The cavalry were in confusion; they evidently could not, with all the weight of man and horse, penetrate that compact mass of human beings, and their sabres were plied to hew a way through naked held-up hands and defenceless heads; and then chopped limbs and wound-gapping skulls were seen; and groans and cries were mingled with the din of that horrid confusion. . . . By this time Hunt and his companions had disappeared from the hustings, and some of the yeomanry, perhaps less sanguinarily disposed than others, were busied in cutting down the flag-staves and demolishing the flags at the hustings. . . . In ten minutes from the commencement of the havoc the field was an open and almost deserted space.

(S. Bamford, *Passages in the Life of a Radical* (1844), vol. 1, pp. 207–8)

Source C: The Times

The place appointed for the meeting was a large and vacant piece of ground on the north side of St. Peter's Church. About 11.30 the first body of reformers arrived, bearing two banners, each of which was surmounted by a cap of liberty. The first bore the inscription 'Annual Parliaments and Universal Suffrage', on the reverse side, 'No Corn Laws'. The others said the same with the addition 'Vote by ballot'. . . . Numerous reformers continued to arrive until one o'clock from different towns in the neighbourhood of Manchester. . . . The reformers demeaned themselves becomingly, though a posse of 300 constables had marched into the field about 12, unsupported by any military body. Not the slightest insult was offered them.

Part of the procession was of the Oldham Female Reform Club and whilst we were internally pitying the delusion which led them to a scene so ill-suited to their usual habits, a group of the women of Manchester, attracted by the crowd, came to the corner of the street. They viewed these female reformers for some time and at last burst out, 'Go home to your families and leave such matters to your husbands and sons who better understand them'. The women who thus addressed them were of the lower order in life.

(*The Times*, Thursday 19 August 1819)

Source D: The Times – editorial

Whatever may have been the preliminary circumstances connected with the assembly, whatever may be our sense of the merits of those who promoted it – of their political principles, of the unfitness of the season at which 50,000 people, half employed and half starved, were congregated to a single spot to be puffed up by prodigious notions of their strength and inflamed by artful pictures of their grievances – all such considerations sink to nothing before the dreadful fact that nearly 100 of the King's unarmed subjects have been sabred by cavalry in the streets of their own town, in the presence of those Magistrates whose sworn duty it is to preserve the life of the meanest Englishman.

(Ibid.)

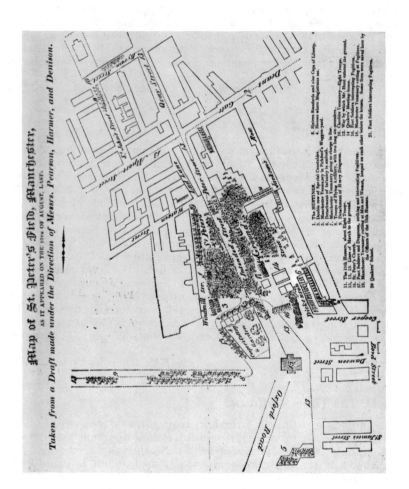

Figure 3.3

Source F: Rev. Edward Stanley

At length Hunt made his appearance in an open barouche . . . on reaching the hustings which were prepared for the orator, he was received with enthusiastic applause. . . . He began to address them. . . . About this time there was an alarm among the women and children near the place where I stood, and I could also see a part of the crowd in motion towards the Deansgate side, but I thought it a false alarm, as many returned again and joined in the huzzas of the crowd. A second alarm arose, and I heard the sound of a horn and immediately the Manchester Yeomanry appeared. . . . I heard the order to form three deep and then the order to march. The trumpeter led the way and galloped towards the hustings, followed by the yeomanry. . . . Their sabres glistened in the air, and on they went, direct for the hustings. . . . As the cavalry approached the dense mass of people, they used their utmost efforts to escape; but so closely were they pressed in opposite directions by the soldiers, the special constables, the position of the hustings and their own immense numbers, that immediate escape was impossible. . . . The Manchester Yeomanry had already taken possession of the hustings, when the Cheshire Yeomanry entered on my left in excellent order and formed in the rear of the hustings . . . the Fifteenth Dragoons appeared nearly at the same moment, and paused rather than halted on our left, parallel to the row of houses. They then pressed forward, crossing the avenue of constables, which opened to let them through, and set their course towards the Manchester Yeomanry. The people were now in a state of utter rout and confusion. . . . The cavalry were hurrying about in all directions, completing the work of dispersion. . . . I saw nothing that gave me an idea of resistance . . . The whole of this extraordinary scene was the work of a few minutes.
(Evidence of Rev. E. Stanley in F. Bruton (ed.), 'Three Accounts of Peterloo', 1921, printed in P. Hollis, *Class and Conflict in Nineteenth-Century England 1815–1850*, 1973, pp. 99–101)

Source G: Francis Philips

I shall give a verbatim copy of a narrative I wrote at the request of a friend about six weeks ago. . . . I mixed with the crowd, where pressures appeared the least, and was at one time within twenty-five yards of the hustings, on the side nearest to the Magistrates. Although no direct affront was offered me, the observations, boldly and tauntingly made, convinced me of the revolutionary tendency of the meeting, and that they were confident of eventually overturning the Government. . . . The Yeomanry . . . proceeded at a slow pace, it appeared to me, in file; but from the numbers before me, I could not see distinctly. I was alarmed for their safety. . . . Whilst near me, I did not see a sword used, and I solemnly declare my firm belief that, if the crowd had given way to them, no cuts would have been given; a great dust arose when they quickened their speed, so that I could not distinguish all that passed, but certainly I did not see one person struck with the sabre.
(F. Philips, *An Exposure of the Calumnies Circulated by the Enemies of Social Order*, November 1819)

Source H: Lt.-Colonel L'Estrange

Early in the afternoon, the civil power finding it necessary that the troops should act in aid of them, it was deemed expedient that the cavalry should advance; and a warrant was executed . . . under which two persons Hunt and Johnson, named therein were arrested. . . . This service was performed with the assistance of the cavalry. The infantry was in readiness, but I determined not to bring them in contact with the people, unless compelled to do so by urgent necessity; not a shot therefore has been fired by the populace against the troops. I have, however, great regret in stating that some of the unfortunate people who attended this meeting have suffered from sabre wounds, and many from the pressures of the crowd.

(Report to General Sir John Byng written around 8 o'clock that evening, printed in Paper Relative to the Internal State of the Country, November 1819, pp. 30–1)

Historians must know the range and types of sources available to them. It is not a matter of identifying the most important sources and then 'squeezing' them fully but using a variety of different evidence that has a bearing on the issue under consideration. G. R. Elton has argued that historical analysis means 'an exhaustive, and exhausting, review of everything that may conceivably be germane to a given investigation'. Where the material is of manageable proportions this is not really a problem. But as historians approach the present day so the bulk of material increases. No one historian can cover everything.

There were good and bad contemporary witnesses, good and bad judges of people and events between whom historians must distinguish. But their judgements are valid only if they are grounded in evidence that has been critically tested. Historians must always be sceptical. It is in that scepticism and critical method that the historian's objectivity lies.

Further work

You should relate the questions below to the specific topics and periods you are studying.

(1) How far does primary evidence allow historians to tell 'the truth' about the past?

(2) Why is 'selection' a problem for historians?

(3) Distinguish between 'fair comment', 'bias' and 'prejudice'. Why is this distinction important and how does it affect the way historians approach primary evidence?

(4) Historical objectivity lies in the critical examination of evidence upon which plausible interpretations can be grounded. Discuss.

(5) Assess the validity of T. E. Lawrence's assertion that 'documents are liars'.

(6) Historians through evidence and their writings based on its examination create the past. Discuss.

4 Primary Sources – Written and Printed

Historians cannot too frequently remind themselves that their material is not the enormously dense networks of actual human relations in the past, but only the fragmented surviving record from which they may be able to elicit some sense of some of the intelligible patterns and structures that once were part of that network.
(J. H. Hexter, *The History Primer*, Allen Lane, 1972)

In addition, Robert Rhodes James clearly expressed one of the historian's major problems when writing of the Chanak incident of 1922:

In any crisis of this nature the historian, however well equipped with information, is at a disadvantage. Any crisis generates its own momentum and its own personality. The stress of events; fragmentary information; the characters of individual ministers; physical tiredness; sheer chance: all these play their part, and contribute to the character and development of the crisis to an extent of which even the participants are often unaware. And thus it is that follies are committed and a sense of proportion lost for reasons which are impossible to specify with any exactness. Thus, however complete the documentation may be, the true causes are usually absent.
(R. R. James, *Churchill: A Study in Failure, 1900–1939* (Weidenfeld & Nicolson, 1970)

And, as G. R. Elton put it, there is 'the unexpected, the unforeseen, the contingent, the accidental and the unknowable'.

We are exploring two contrasting aspects of history in this chapter: the political parties of the later Stuart period, and European imperialism in Africa in the late nineteenth century. The rich diversity of primary written and printed source material should be evident in both sections, with sources drawn from private and public collections. To what extent are these documents compiled for personal or public reasons? Were they written with the future reader in mind, striving to justify a particular course of action or to exculpate the writer? Are they of polemical interest, as in a political speech, or propaganda? How do examples from one part of a country illuminate national, even international, issues? What is the standpoint of the writer? Can we hear the 'buzzing' of his point of view, as E. H. Carr said?

Selection is another problem: how have the documents been selected and by whom? Can subjectivity in their selection be detected? What questions should be asked of the documents, and how can they develop our knowledge and insight into the period being studied? As Martin Gilbert said, 'Evidence is something you play with as a kitten plays with a ball of wool.'

1. Political Parties and Elections, 1689–1714

Letters from country gentlemen to those involved in government at the centre convey the problems and distortions created by inadequate news, even for literate and intelligent men. What do these letters suggest of politics in the provinces?

(a) A Suffolk Squire

We have for some time expected a dissolution of this Parliament, but if the Lord Lieutenants of some counties be not turned out, and particularly ours, matters will not go so well as we wish. Our Duke tells us the Pretender is coming, and my Lord Hervey is very much dissatisfied at the present ministry. One of Bury Corporation asked a favour of his Lordship. He answered he would not ask anything of this ministry; and if no other Lord in the House would join with him, he himself would move to have the successor sent for. The man seemeth to be very angry and expressed his anger very much. Many witty things were said against our friends. He says a worse thing could not be done than turning out my Lord Godolphin. Pray let us have my Lord Dysart for our Lord Lieutenant again which will make our country happy.

Another thing the noble Duke said, that our friends are sorry for the victory in Spain, and that we have no religion and are not for a peace. . . .
(Sir Robert Davers to Robert Harley, 6 September 1710, HMC 29 Portland V, p. 590)

(b) A Country Peer

My very good friend, nothing is so acceptable to a country gentleman like myself than to hear from my friends in town. . . .

I sit and philosophize over your *Réflexions Curieuses*, and in the main am come to this point, that my books, my garden, and my two little rooms over my greenhouse are my best tenure. And for one that has neither superstition nor more religion than is absolutely necessary, a quiet mind is better than to embroil, plague and trouble myself amongst the kn—s and fo—ls about either Church or State. . . .

But to leave politics, I desire Cavalier Davie would let me know what size he must have the stone got for his double figures, for should we go on with the design of his cutting the figures for my garden, I am in hopes I can find stone here, which will not only save the charge of carriage, but will also secure us from any breach or damage by so long a way of carriage as is from London hither. Pray let me know this in your next, and as anything new either at home or abroad happens, oblige your country friend with it, who cannot go to the price of Mr. Dyer [author of a Tory newsletter] and therefore am quite ignorant how matters go.
(The Earl of Cholmondeley to Matthew Prior, 6 August 1710, HMC 58 Bath III, pp. 438–9)

(c) Christmas in Buckinghamshire

Our house is every day very full of Country People, that it's like an Election time. It quite tires me which makes me wish the Christmas were over. I don't hear that any of your Sister Verney's tickets are yet drawn, they are still in the Wheel and worth near 15 shillings a Ticket. . . .

Dear Ralph, – I have now 2 Tenants come to tell me, they will leave at Lady Day unless I will abate of the Rent, tho' the present Rents have been these 50 years and above. I am very glad Christmas is ended, for we have had every day a vast number of people, but my servants say here were 400 people and I do believe there were rather more last Tuesday. It has been a troublesome time; every day with the noise of either drums, trumpets, hautboys, pipes or fiddles, some days 400 guests, very few under 100, that besides the vast expense it has been very tiresome. I wish all your family a happy New Year. This last night a fit of the gout took me in the foot, which confines me to my chair for I can't go about the room. Lady F.'s tickets are now all come out Blanks, your Sister I believe hath 2 still in the Wheel.

(Lord Fermanagh to Ralph Verney, 31 December 1712, and 8 January 1713,
Verney Letters, p. 291)

With the active politicians, like the Davers of Rushbrooke, Suffolk, and the Verneys of Claydon, Buckinghamshire, news of who was in or out, rising and falling, was meat and drink. Elections – held at least once every three years under the Triennial Act of 1694 – were a source of great activity and excitement for voters and non-voters alike. The next group of documents refers to these elections, with questions at the end.

(d) Motives of Electors

What chiefly inclines the electors, in the preference of the persons to represent them, is the opinion they have of the good dispositions of such persons to serve them and their country by voting and speaking for their nation's good. This, their good opinion of men, will arise in different persons from very different reasons: in some in that they, by themselves or friends, receive some advantages or favours, or have some dependence in point of interest upon them whom they elect. But the most popular reason, and so of greatest use in the counties, cities and great boroughs, where the right of election is in the populace, is an opinion that the persons elected will endeavour the security of the religion they profess and the properties they enjoy. And for this reason men that differ in religion and interest so often disagree about the persons they would elect.

(Anonymous, *Occasional Thoughts concerning our Present Divisions and their Remedies*, 1704, pp. 10–11)

(e) Nonconformist Votes

I told you in my last that there was a messenger sent to Mil[denh]all and that side, and accordingly there was. Mr. Glascock was not at home, Captain Pamplin was engaged to Sir Robert Davers, and so was Mr. Judd; he told the messenger his brother Wright was not at home but he believed he was engaged. . . .

Some of the dissenters came to me at Bury some time before the Parliament broke up, and told me it was a prejudice to your interest if you did not apply yourself to Mr. Bury and Mr. Snelling and some others of the heads of the party. . . . Mr. Smith in a company where I met him yesterday openly declared that Sir R. Davers was utterly against taking off the Toleration, and therefore I think if the Dissenters had some application made to them it were not amiss.

[Pitches was Sir Dudley Cullum's Chaplain]

> (Mr Pitches to Sir Dudley Cullum, 30 May 1702, West Suffolk Record Office
> Cullum Correspondence, E2/18/162)

(f) Buckinghamshire Elections

My Lord – I have been several times at Westminster since the Parliament met, with design to speak to your Lordship that you would be favourable and kind to send the Votes, the Post Boy and Post Man to Sherrington, at the Crown in Chesham, Postmaster, as your Lordship did last Session of Parliament. He has a Club of your friends meet every Friday at his house, who will desert for want of hearing from their friends. Sir Edmund Denton furnished another house most plentifully, out of Parliament as well as in during all the last Summer.

> (Viscount Cheyne to Lord Fermanagh, 18 December 1711, *Verney Letters*, p. 308)

Hearing that your Lordship is in town I give you the trouble of a letter to acquaint you with the reason that induced me to stand at Buckingham, where my carrying it is very doubtful, for that Corporation hath but 13 electors and my Cousin Denton lives so near 'em that the Loaves sway much with them. I well remember at the last County Election several, and amongst others Sir Roger Hill, asked me, why I did not stand at Buckm., seeing that townsfolk come in so unanimously for me; but I answered that Sir Richd. Temple and Alex Dent[o]n were the late Members and both my Kinsm[e]n, and that I thought it not handsome to endeavour to jostle either of them out; but now there is a vacancy by death I put in for it, else they would say twas pride in me that I would be a K[nigh]t of the Shire only, whereas I might be a Burgess for asking.

> (Lord Fermanagh to Viscount Cheyne, February 1712, op. cit., p. 309)

(g) Wooing the Electors

I am but a Stranger in the Land, and know the Chiltern can cut the Vale [of Aylesbury] out five to one as to number of Electors, yet I have heard, the Vale do at all times think it hard if One of their Kn[igh]ts be not of their part of the Country.

> (Sir John Verney to Sir Roger Hill, 17 July 1698, *Verney Letters*, p. 155)

I am informed on all hands how sedulous my Sister was in managing her part as to the Pleasing all the Freeholders that came to the House; and her Art is so much extolled in the Chiltern, that all persons say no one could have better acted her part . . . and Mrs. Fleetwood also did tell me they want mightily to see her in the Chiltern that they may all return her and my Lord their thanks for the same.

> (Daniel Baker to Ralph Verney, 7 October 1710, *Verney Letters*, p. 303)

(h) Election Propaganda

The cry of the Whiggish rabble at the election for the county of Chester during the election was 'Down with the Church and the Bishops'; and when about 60 of the clergy headed by the Dean came to poll they said Hell was broke loose and these were the Devil's black guard; they abused the Bishop . . . and . . . broke the windows of the Cathedral and another church.

> (*Dyer's News Letter*, 29 May 1705 in HMC 29 Portland IV p. 189)

(i) 1710 Election in Buckinghamshire

Bucks. Lord Fermanagh	2161
Sir Ed. Denton	2157
Mr. Hampden	2148
Sir Harry Seymour	2099

(*The Post-Man*, 10–11 October 1710, Nicols Newspapers, 356ᵛ, Bodleian Library, Oxford)

By letters from Buckinghamshire, it appears that Mr. Hampden lost his Election there, not for want of Interest, but by his Friends being too secure, which made great Numbers of 'em stay at home, because they thought there was no need of 'em; besides, 23 Freeholders, that were actually on their Way to Vote for him, were unhappily prevented by a false Report, from one whom they did not mistrust, that the Books were shut up before they were. After all, he lost it by a small Majority, as may be seen by the Poll.

(*The Flying-Post*, 10–12 October 1710)

(j) 'Honest Tom' Wharton

No General Election was quite complete unless virtually every constituency had received a visit from . . . [Lord Wharton] in company with his celebrated gang. . . . [At High Wycombe during one election campaign] my Lord entering a shoemaker's shop, asks where Dick was? The good woman said, her husband was gone two or three miles off with some shoes, but his Lordship need not fear him, she would keep him tight; I know that, says my Lord, but I want to see Dick, and drink a glass with him. The wife was very sorry Dick was out of the way, well, says his Lordship, how does all the children; Molly is a brave girl I warrant by this time? Yes, I thank ye my Lord, says the woman, and his Lordship continued, Is not Jemmy breeched yet?

A friend of one of the Tory candidates, observing all this, cried to his colleague, 'E'en take your horse and be gone, whoever has my Lord Wharton on his side, has enough for his Election.'

(Sir Richard Steele, *Memoirs of the Life . . . of Thomas, late Marquess of Wharton*, 1715)

(k) 1710: The Result

6 October 1710

We now hear daily of elections, and in a list I saw yesterday of about twenty, there are seven or eight more Tories than in the last parliament; so that I believe they need not fear a majority, with the help of those who will vote as the Court pleases. But I have been told that Mr. Harley himself would not let the Tories be too numerous, for fear they should be insolent, and kick against him.

(Jonathan Swift, *Journal to Stella*, ed. H. Williams, Oxford, 1974, I, p. 52)

In conjunction with the Buckinghamshire pollbook example from Chapter 5, these documents offer a varied outlook on elections. What do they suggest about:

(1) The changed meaning of 'interest' and 'engaged'?

(2) The importance of religion?

(3) Party organisation?

(4) Why men voted as they did?

(5) Election propaganda?

(6) Party management at the centre and in the constituencies?

(7) The validity of Lord Hervey's comment of 1710 that 'I need not tell you what coy mistresses boroughs are, and that they never were more courted than at present.'

How significant may be the alteration made to a document by modern English, revised punctuation or omissions (indicated by three dots)? Consider Martin Gilbert: 'I am a severe critic of the three dot brigade. One has constantly to make the decision where to end the quotation, but I have formed a rule: never take something out of the middle of a sentence.'

Finally, Henry St John (Viscount Bolingbroke) on the Tory aims of 1710:

(1) A Politician Reflects

I am afraid that we came to court in the same dispositions as all parties have done; that the principal spring of our actions was to have the government of the state in our hands; that our principal views were the conservation of this power, great
5   employments to ourselves, and great opportunities of rewarding those who had helped to raise us, and of hurting those who stood in opposition to us. It is, however, true, that with these considerations of private and party interest there were others intermingled, which had for their object the public
10   good of the nation, at least what we took to be such.
We looked on the political principles which had generally prevailed in our government from the Revolution in one thousand six hundred and eighty-eight, to be destructive of our true interest, to have mingled us too much in the affairs
15   of the Continent, to tend to the impoverishing our people, and to the loosening the bands of our constitution in Church and State. We supposed the Tory party to be the bulk of the landed interest, and to have no contrary influence blended into its composition. We supposed the Whigs to be the remains of a
20   party, formed against the ill designs of the Court under King Charles the second, nursed up into strength and applied to contrary uses by King William the third, and yet still so weak as to lean for support on the Presbyterians and other sectaries, on the Bank and the other corporations, on the
25   Dutch and the other allies. From hence we judged it to follow that they had been forced, and must continue so, to render the national interest subservient to the interest of those who lent them an additional strength, without which they could never be the prevalent party. The view, therefore, of those amongst us
30   who thought in this manner, was to improve the Queen's favour to break the body of the Whigs, to render their supports useless to them, and to fill the employment of the kingdom, down to the

meanest, with Tories. We imagined that such measures, joined to
the advantages of our numbers and property, would secure us
35   against all attempts during her reign; and that we should soon
become too considerable not to make our terms in all events
which might happen afterwards; concerning which, to speak
truly, I believe few or none of us had any very settled resolution.

(A Letter to Sir William Windham, 1753, pp. 19–22)

Why might this be considered an unusual statement from a politician of any
historical period? How would the tone of this document be altered by
omitting lines 7–29, as one textbook writer did?

2. The Scramble for Africa

The second section deals with an extra-European topic, introducing a British
historian to additional problems of different languages and cultures. Perhaps
there are also feelings of post-colonial guilt, or concern about the 'North–
South' economic divide of the late twentieth century; or even doubts about
the value of this study: one famous British historian wrote that we cannot
afford to 'amuse ourselves with the unrewarding gyrations of barbarous
tribes in picturesque but irrelevant corners of the globe'.

An essentially oral society is one that may have lapsed after previous
greatness but there is no proof of this because there are so few written – and
no printed – documents. Many sceptical explorers, for example, questioned
whether the impressive ruins of Great Zimbabwe were really African in
origin.

(a) Explorer's Africa

Central Africa . . . is without a history. In that savage country . . . we find no
vestiges of the past – no ancient architecture, neither sculpture, nor even one chiselled
stone to prove that the Negro savage of this day is inferior to a remote ancestor. . . .
We must therefore conclude that the races of man which now inhabit [this region] are
unchanged from the prehistoric tribes who were the original inhabitants.

(Sir Samuel Baker, 1874, in M. E. Chamberlain, The Scramble for Africa,
Longman, 1974, p. 3)

Sir Bartle Frere agreed,

If you read the history of any part of the Negro population of Africa, you will find
nothing but a dreary recurrence of tribal wars, and an absence of everything which
forms a stable government, and year after year, generation after generation, century
after century, these tribes go on obeying no law but that of force, and consequently
never emerging from the state of barbarism in which we find them at present, and in
which they have lived, so far as we know, for a period long anterior to our own.

(Ibid.)

There is also a tendency to rationalise events involving Europeans and to ignore the indigenous point of view. After all, where was the evidence for the Third World's reaction to European conquest? As one historian ironically wrote in 1975, 'Europeans are . . . always the agents of rationality and modernization, while Africans and Asians represent conservative "pre-capitalist" modes of behaviour.' And George Kitson Clark wrote that 'to be significant history must choose from the mass of the records of what has happened those facts which relate to a particular issue or group of issues or which gain their meaning from a particular calculus of values. And there is no reason why these reference points should be the same for all individuals in all generations.'

Thirdly, Paul Kennedy suggested that 'today's anti-nationalist historians exhibit some of the faults and weaknesses of their more chauvinist forebears. Types of prejudice may change: the existence of prejudice remains.'

(b) Imperialism

Two ideas of imperialism can be seen in works of fiction by Joseph Conrad and George Bernard Shaw.

> The conquest of the earth, which mostly means the taking it away from those who have a different complexion or slightly flatter noses than ourselves, is not a pretty thing when you look into it too much. What redeems it is the idea only. An idea at the back of it: not a sentimental pretence but an idea; and an unselfish belief in the idea – something you can set up, and bow down before, and offer a sacrifice to.
>
> (Marlow in *The Heart of Darkness*, Joseph Conrad)

> Every Englishman is born with a certain miraculous power that makes him master of the world. When he wants a thing he never tells himself that he wants it. He waits patiently till there comes into his head, no one knows how, the burning conviction that it is his moral and religious duty to conquer those who have the thing he wants. Then he becomes irresistible. Like the aristocrat he does what pleases him and grabs what he wants; like the shopkeeper he pursues his purpose with the industry and steadfastness that come from strong religious conviction and deep sense of moral responsibility. He is never at a loss for an effective moral attitude. As the great champion of freedom and independence, he conquers half the world and calls it Colonization. When he wants a new market for his adulterated Manchester goods, he sends a missionary to teach the gospel of peace. The natives kill the missionary; he flies to arms in defence of Christianity; fights for it, conquers for it; and takes the market as a reward from heaven.
>
> (G. B. Shaw, *The Man of Destiny*)

How could an historian use these ideas? What would he want to know of the authors? Are these extracts good history or good literature?

(c) The Lure of Profit

There was also the lure of unknown regions:

Most of the country from the Tanganyika to the West Coast is one of almost unspeakable richness. Of metals, there are iron, copper, silver and gold; coal is also found; the vegetable products are palm-oil, cotton, nutmegs, besides several sorts of pepper and coffee, all growing wild. The people cultivate several other oil-producing plants, such as ground-nuts and seni seni. The Arabs, as far as they have come, have introduced rice, wheat, onions, and a few fruit trees, all of which seem to flourish well. The countries of Bihé and Bailunda are sufficiently high above the sea to be admirably adapted for European occupation, and would produce whatever may be grown in the south of Europe. . . . To the eastward of Lovalé ivory is marvellously plentiful. The price among the Arab traders at Nyangwé was 7½ pounds of beads, or 5 pounds of cowries, for 35 pounds of ivory; and the caravans that went out from there for ivory would obtain tusks, irrespective of weight, for an old knife, a copper bracelet, or any other useless thing which might take the fancy of the natives.

(Lieutenant Cameron's report to the Royal Geographical Society, April 1876; *Proceedings of the Royal Geographical Society*, 1st ser., xx, 323–4 in Chamberlain op. cit., p. 105)

'I contend that we are the first race in the world and the more of the world we inhabit the better it is for the human race' (Cecil Rhodes). By 1900 the British empire consisted of 400 million people occupying one-fifth of the globe; France controlled 52 million people over 6 million square miles. Traders and politicians used several arguments to emphasise the importance of pre-emptive colonisation:

(d) Being there First

The effect of a Portuguese extension [in West Africa] would be to exterminate the British trade existing in the absorbed territory, as it could not exist under the grinding exactions of a protective Customs Tariff, which would practically prohibit the importation of every manufacture of British origin. A writer who lived for many years in Angola, and who had abundant opportunities of witnessing the miserable state to which that fine country had been reduced by the wretched and corrupt system of government, represents Portuguese rule there as a 'despotic oppression that crushed the whole country under its heel, depopulating it, and stifling any attempt at industrial development'. . . .

France of late years has been making vigorous efforts to extend her influence in Western Africa. . . . If France sets so high a value on her future in Africa as to deem it wise to extend her power, and to accept gladly the responsibilities of an enlarged empire, and if Portugal does not shrink from the additional cares of an increased territory, it is reasonable to hope that England will not allow the trade at present possessed by her to be confiscated for the benefit of protectionist competitors; but that the influence due to her by virtue of her great colonial and trading interests in Western Africa, which far exceed those of all other nations combined, will be maintained, and, if necessary, her territory extended, in order to prevent the encroachments of foreign powers whose interests are antagonistic to those of Great Britain.

(John Holt, Liverpool, to Lord Granville, 11 December 1882, Granville Papers, Public Record Office, P.R.O. 30/29/269 in Chamberlain op. cit., p. 121)

(e) French Colonialism

I repeat that the superior races have a right because they have a duty. They have a duty to civilise the inferior races. And then there is the political aspect of the matter. M. Pelletan said 'It is a system which amounts to seeking compensation in the East for the caution and self-containment which are at the moment imposed on us in Europe'. Now I must make it plain that I do not like this word compensation. . . . There can be no compensation, none whatever, for the disasters we have suffered. . . . The real question which has to be asked, and clearly asked, is this: must the containment forced on nations which experience great misfortunes result in abdications? . . . Are [French governments] going to remain just as spectators and allow people other than ourselves in Tunisia, allow people other than ourselves to police the mouth of the Red River and fulfil the clauses of the treaty of 1874, which we undertook to get respected in the interests of European nations? Are they going to leave it to others to dispute the mastery of the regions of equatorial Africa? Are they going to leave it to others to decide the affairs of Egypt which, from so many points of view, are in reality French affairs? I assert that France's colonial policy, the policy of colonial expansion – that policy which sent us during the period of the Empire to Saigon and Cochin China, which led us to Tunisia, which drew us to Madagascar: I make bold to say that this policy of colonial expansion was based on a truth of which for a moment I must remind you. This is that our navy and merchant shipping in their business on the high seas must have safe harbours, defence positions and supply points.

(Jules Ferry to the French Chamber of Deputies, arguing in favour of further French involvement in Madagascar, 28 July 1885)

Can you identify the aspects of French foreign and colonial policy during the nineteenth century revealed by Ferry? How much of the tone of both these documents amounts to special pleading or arguments for popular consumption?

(f) Partition

In 1884–5 the Berlin West Africa Conference introduced guidelines for annexation. What is noteworthy about the style of this extract?

Chapter I. The Congo
Article 1
The trade of all nations shall enjoy complete freedom –
   1. In all the regions forming the basin of the Congo and its outlets.
   2. In the maritime zone extending along the Atlantic Ocean from the Parallel situated in 2° 30' of south latitude to the mouth of the Logé. . . .
Article 6
All the powers exercising sovereign rights or influence in the aforesaid territories bind themselves to watch over the preservation of the native tribes, and to care for the improvement of the conditions of their moral and material well-being, and to help in suppressing slavery, and especially the Slave Trade. They shall, without distinction of creed or nation, protect and favour all religions, scientific or charitable institutions, and undertakings created and organised for the above ends, or which aim at instructing the natives and bringing home to them the blessings of civilization. Christian missionaries, scientists, and explorers, with their followers, property, and collections, shall likewise be the objects of special protection. . . .
Chapter VI. New Occupations

Article 34

Any Power which henceforth takes possession of a tract of land on the coasts of the African Continent outside of its present possessions, or which, being hitherto without such possessions, shall acquire them, as well as the Power which assumes a protectorate there, shall accompany the respective act with a notification thereof, addressed to the other Signatory Powers of the present Act, in order to enable them, if need be, to make good any claim of their own.

> (General Act of the Berlin Conference on West Africa, signed on 26 February 1885, *Parliamentary Papers*, lv (1884–5), 438 in Chamberlain op. cit., pp. 124–5)

The Partition could also be used as an element of European power politics – 'the extension into the periphery of the political struggle in Europe' as D. K. Fieldhouse wrote – and Egypt was a prime example of this. Note the use by Bismarck in the third document here of the *bâton égyptien* against Britain.

(g) Suez Canal

Mr. Disraeli with his humble duty to Yr. Majesty

The Khedive, on the eve of bankruptcy, appears desirous of parting with his shares in the Suez Canal, & has communicated, confidentially, with General Stanton. There is a French company in negotiation with His Highness, but they purpose only to make an advance with complicated stipulations.

'Tis an affair of millions; about four, at least but wo^d give the possessor an immense, not to say preponderating, influence in the management of the Canal.

It is vital to Her Majesty's authority & power at this critical moment, that the Canal should belong to England. . . . The Cabinet was unanimous in their decision, that the interests of the Khedive sh^d., if possible, be obtained. . . .

The Khedive now says, that it is absolutely necessary that he should have between three & four millions sterling by the 30th. of this month!

Scarcely breathing time! But the thing must be done. . . .

> (Disraeli to the Queen, 18 November 1875, P.R.O. CAB 41/6/33, in 'You have it, Madam', Lord Rothschild, 1980, pp. 15–16)

Mr. Disraeli with his humble duty to Yr Majesty.

It is just settled: you have it, Madam. The French Government has been outgeneraled. They tried too much, offering loans at an usurious rate, & with conditions wh: would have virtually given them the government of Egypt.

The Khedive, in despair & disgust, offered Yr Majesty's Government to purchase his shares outright – he never would listen to such a proposition before.

Four millions sterling! and almost immediately. There was only one firm that cd do it – Rothschilds. They behaved admirably; advanced the money at a low rate, and the entire interest of the Khedive is now yours, Madam.

> (Disraeli to the Queen, 24 November 1875, Royal Archives A.50, in Rothschild, op. cit., p. 20)

(h) The Egyptian Baton

. . . Count Bismarck spoke to me at length today by order of the Chancellor on the subject [of Zanzibar]. . . .

He reverted to the subject now because he once more asked for the assistance and friendly action of H.M.'s Govt in the matter of Zanzibar. In return for that he would reject all the ouvertures which might be made to him by the new French ambassador to help France in embarrassing us in Egypt and in all questions in which our interests and those of France were in divergence, he would not only refuse to go against us but would give us such assistance as might be possible consistently with the necessities of his home position.

(Malet to Iddesleigh, 2 October 1886, F.O. 244/415/71 in C. J. Lowe, *The Reluctant Imperialists*, II, 1967, pp. 63–4)

James Joll once referred to politicians in moments of crisis falling back 'on their instinctive reactions, traditions and modes of behaviour. Each of them has certain beliefs, rules or objectives which are taken for granted; and one of the limitations of documentary evidence is that few people bother to write down, especially in moments of crisis, things which they take for granted.' These are the 'unspoken assumptions' which may have their origins in such things as a person's education, or the climate of opinion of his youth. The famous explorer H. M. Stanley wrote this in 1890; its title is, perhaps, significant, but what does it reveal about Stanley's attitude to the native population?

(i) Social Darwinism?

. . . Villages were seen nestling amid abundance, and we left them unmolested in the hope that the wild people might read that when left alone we were an extremely inoffensive band of men. But at nine o'clock . . . we heard the first war-cries. . . . By 11 a.m. there were two separate bands of natives who followed us very persistently. . . .

By noon these bands had increased into numerous and frantic mobs, and some of them cried out, 'We will prove to you before night that we are men, and every one of you shall perish today. . . .' The mobs followed us, now and then making demonstrations, and annoying us with their harsh cries and menaces. An expert shot left the line of march, and wounded two of them at a range of 400 yards. This silenced them for a while. . . .

To punish them for four hours persecution of us we turned about and set fire to every hut on either bank. . . . It should be observed that up to the moment of firing the villages, the fury of the natives seemed to be increasing, but the instant the flames were seen devouring their homes the fury ceased, by which we learned that fire had a remarkable sedative influence on their nerves.

(H. M. Stanley, *In Darkest Africa*, 1890, I, pp. 299–300, in Chamberlain op. cit., pp. 107–8)

(David Livingstone expressed a very different view in 1865: 'In reference to the status of the Africans among the nations of the earth, we have seen nothing to justify the notion that they are of a different "breed" or "species" from the most civilized. The African is a man with every attribute of human kind.')

The Congo Report on the scandalous nature of King Leopold's company in that area was very concerned about the natives. Was this because Leopold had been excessive even by European standards?

(j) The Congo Scandal

[A village native of the Congo in reply to Casement's question how much they were paid for rubber-picking] 'Our village got cloth and a little salt, but not the people who did the work. Our chiefs ate up the cloth: the workers got nothing. The pay was a fathom of cloth and a little salt for every big basketful, but it was given to the chief, never to the men. It used to take ten days to get twenty baskets of rubber – we were always in the forest, and then when we were late we were killed. We had to go farther and farther into the forest to find the rubber vines, to go without food, and our women had to give up cultivating the fields and gardens. Then we starved. Wild beasts – the leopards – killed some of us when we were working away in the forest, and others got lost or died from exposure and starvation, and we begged the white man to leave us alone, saying we could get no more rubber, but the white men and their soldiers said: 'Go! You are only beasts yourselves. . . .'

We tried, always going farther into the forest, and when we failed and our rubber was short, the soldiers came to our towns and killed us. Many were shot, some had their ears cut off; others were tied up with ropes around their necks and bodies and taken away. The white men sometimes at the posts did not know of the bad things the soldiers did to us, but it was the white men who sent the soldiers to punish us for not bringing in enough rubber.' [Casement reported] when I visited the three mud huts which serve the purpose of the native hospital [in Leopoldville], all of them dilapidated, and two with the thatched roofs almost gone, I found seventeen sleeping sickness patients, male and female, lying about in the utmost dirt. Most of them were lying on the bare ground – several out on the pathway in front of the houses, and one, a woman, had fallen into the fire just prior to my arrival and had burned herself very badly. . . . In somewhat striking contrast to the neglected state of these people, I found, within a couple of hundred yards of them, the government workshop for repairing and fitting the steamers. Here all was brightness, care, order, and activity, and it was impossible not to admire and commend the industry which had created and maintained in constant working order this useful establishment.

(Roger Casement, 'Congo Report to the Marquess of Lansdowne', 11 December 1903 in *The Black Diaries*, P. Singleton-Gates and M. Girodias)

As Hilaire Belloc said, 'We have the Maxim gun, and they have not'! Or, unfortunately for the historian, it is how the literate overcame the illiterate, and were able to present their view in the sources. Only recently have Africans begun to write their own history, although not always with historical truth in mind. (This problem of sources is also acute in other countries – especially in obtaining primary evidence on Chinese history.)

We also have to recognise the *Weltanschauung* of contemporaries: how their perception of people and events – even of history – differed from ours. (And when we say 'ours' do we mean teenagers or people in their forties or seventies?) 'Social Darwinism', a crude simplification of Charles Darwin's theories on the origin of species, was prevalent in the late nineteenth century, and may be recognised in several of the documents in this section.

The historian has also to cope with foreign languages – European certainly. What did King Leopold of the Belgians mean when he said in 1886: 'La richesse et la prospérité des peuples ne tiennent pas à une seule enterprise, et ne sauraient venir d'une seule contrée. Il faut travailler partout, ne négliger aucune chance, aucune veine . . .'? Or in 1892: 'Pour moi je voudrais faire de notre petite Belgique avec ces six millions d'habitants la capitale d'un immense empire; et cette pensée, il y a moyen de la réaliser. Nous avons le Congo; la Chine en est à la période de décomposition; les Pays-Bas, l'Espagne, le Portugal sont en décadence; leurs colonies seront un jour au plus offrant . . .'?

With the plethora of published source material now available for the historian of the nineteenth and twentieth centuries it is more than ever necessary for him to see the wood for the trees, to learn which documents to select and to ask the right questions. As Neil Tonge and Michael Quincey wrote in *British Social and Economic History 1800–1900* (Macmillan, 1980), 'more and more the student must learn to seek the primary sources, to establish what contemporaries felt to be certainties, to acknowledge bias but to realise that, like all men, they acted on their convictions, prejudices, false assumptions, assessments and all' (p. 6). This chapter should have enabled you to experience some of these problems and opportunities in two aspects of the historical experience.

5   Primary Sources –
Visual, Statistical and Oral

Written and printed sources form only part of the enormous range of evidence available to the historian, who must be equally skilled with visual, statistical and oral evidence.

Visual Evidence

Look at the two drawings from *Contrasts* by Augustus Welby Pugin, published in 1836 (Figure 5.1(a) and (b)). They were drawn to denigrate classical architecture and extol the Gothic style. How did Pugin try to achieve this aim?

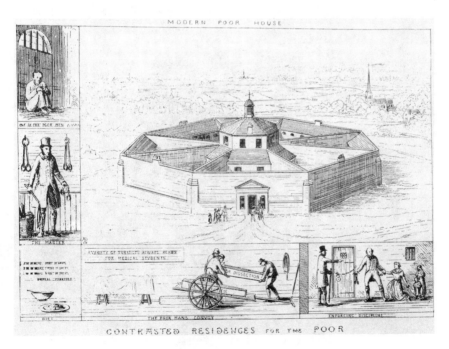

Figure 5.1(a)

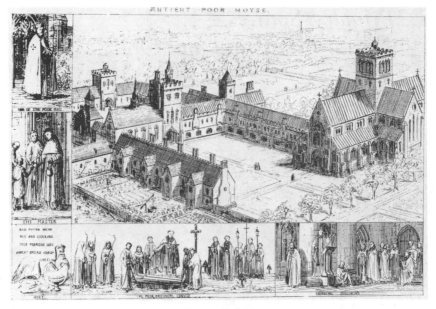

Figure 5.1(b)

Figure 5.2

Figure 5.3

As with written sources the historian must ask who produced the document, when, and why? The paintings of King Charles I by Van Dyck were the creation of an illusion: a serene, imperial and aloof monarch, whose real deficiencies of height and personality were skilfully concealed. Contrast Van Dyck's image of the King resting from the hunt (Figure 5.3) with that of another artist, Mytens (Figure 5.2).

Figure 5.4

John Foxe's *Actes and Monuments*, published in 1563, was a major influence in the development of anti-popery in early modern England; in many churches it was chained alongside the Bible as a source of instruction, and it could also be found in the library of many gentry families. Part of its success lay in the woodcuts which, although crude artistry, added conviction to the textual theme of hostility to Queen Mary Tudor – 'Bloody Mary' (Figures 5.4 and 5.5).

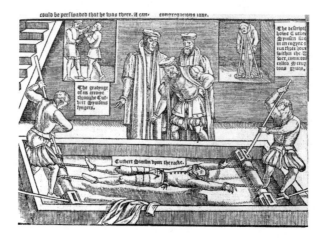

Figure 5.5

The twentieth-century media may be more subtle but the miles of footage of the newsreels of the 1930s show how public opinion was moulded by the five newsreel companies. During the Munich Crisis of 1938, Gaumont-British put forward a view of Prime Minister Neville Chamberlain that was the culmination of several years' work. This transcript attempts to reveal the combination of visual image, commentary and mood music that was so effective at the time.

BBC series script: Unless we understand the significance of [the] cinematographic image of Neville Chamberlain it is impossible to understand either his considerable popularity or the trust he inspired in the hearts of ordinary people, and without this the Munich Crisis of September 1938 would hardly have taken the turn it did.

Gaumont-British, September 1938: The hour of need has found the man, Mr Neville Chamberlain, the Prime Minister. Since he took office Mr Chamberlain has never wavered in his determination to establish peace in Europe. At the hour when the dark clouds of war hung most menacingly above the world of men, the Prime Minister took a wise and bold decision. Well may we call him Chamberlain the Peacemaker. Lord Halifax, the Foreign Secretary, was at Heston to see the Premier off on this epic-making flight to Germany, the first flight he has ever made. We know that no man could do more than he, but since we also know that it lies not in the power of mortals to command success, we say with all our hearts, 'May God go with him!' Three cheers for Chamberlain!. . .

BBC series script: Everything depended at this stage on whether Chamberlain could get and keep the public's support for what was in fact an unprecedented personal deal with a foreign dictator. The newsreels were using the image *they* had built up to justify their giving him unqualified support before the negotiations had even *begun*, let alone succeeded. Years of hard work [by Chamberlain in forging close links with the newsreels and of mastering the technique of creating a cinematic image as the champion of the ordinary man's viewpoint] finally paid off. The Munich Crisis was also the first major crisis covered by the newsreels. British newsreel companies co-operated with the German Ministry of Propaganda to provide massive coverage of Chamberlain's three visits to Hitler. . . . The massive coverage of the crisis provided the cinema audience with a diet of mounting excitement. The now famous newsreel of Chamberlain's return from Munich is both the climax of the media campaign and historical evidence of its result. . . .

As J. A. S. Grenville wrote, 'a piece of film is not some unadulterated reflection of historical truth captured by the camera which does not require the interposition of the historian'. What techniques did the newsreel use to achieve its 'illusion of reality'?

Picture	Commentary	Sound

PEACE INSTEAD OF WAR

Picture	Commentary	Sound
Trenches Cenotaph *On-screen caption:* PEACE. *On-screen caption:* BUT WAS IT PEACE? *On-screen captions,* (Superimposed over film from Manchuria, Abyssinia, Spain and China): 1932 MANCHUKUO 1935 ABYSSINIA 1936 SPAIN 1937 CHINA *On-screen caption:* ONE MAN SAVED US FROM THE GREATEST WAR OF ALL Caption fades into film of Chamberlain at Heston Airport	Twenty-four years ago there was a war to end war. How soon we learned that that was just a dream. 　Millions of young men gave their lives, then the world recovered, but scarcely had the wheels of industry begun to turn again when the house of cards came crashing down once more. 　So our Prime Minister has come back from his third and greatest journey and he said that 'the settlement of the Czechoslovakian problem which has now been achieved is, in my view, only the prelude to a larger settlement in which all Europe may find peace. 　'This morning I had another talk with the German Chancellor, Herr Hitler, and here is the paper which bears his name upon it as well as mine. Some of you, perhaps, have already heard what it contains, but I would just like to read it to you: 　"We, the German Führer and Chancellor, and the British Prime Minister, have had a further meeting today and are agreed in recognising that the question of Anglo-German relations is of the first importance for the two countries and for Europe. We regard the agreement signed last night and the Anglo-German Naval agreement as symbolic of the desire of our two peoples never to go to war with one another again." ' 　There was no sign of British reserve as	'O God, our help in ages past' War sound effects and mood music Cheers Cheers Cheers

Picture	Commentary	Sound

the crowds fought to get near the Premier's car. As we travelled back with Mr Chamberlain from Heston we drove through serried masses of happy people, happy in the knowledge that there was no war with Germany.

Cheers

The Premier drove straight to Buckingham Palace; here he was received by the King while London waited. And history was made again when their Majesties came out on to that famous balcony with the Prime Minister.

Posterity will thank God, as we do now, that in the time of desperate need our safety was guarded by such a man: Neville Chamberlain.

'Land of Hope and Glory'

Illusions of Reality: 2, Men of the Hour, BBC Continuing Education TV written by Nicholas Pronay and produced by Howard Smith

Arthur Marwick identified what he described as 'witting' and 'unwitting testimony': the former is information which the document compiler intended to reveal, while the latter is the assumptions underlying the document. In the newsreel, what unspoken assumptions are there about:

(a) the events of 1938;
(b) the image of Neville Chamberlain;
(c) British politics in the 1930s;
(d) the newsreel company's perception of European history since 1914;
(e) Adolf Hitler and Nazi Germany?

Political cartoons are equally vivid representations of their period. Here is a selection from the twentieth century, and a mid-seventeenth-century one hostile to Oliver Cromwell (Figure 5.9). The one featuring Cromwell has all the hallmarks of the period: a reasonably accurate portrayal of Cromwell, but the rest is emblems and devices: some in Latin (the King James's *Bible*; *Magna Charta*), one in Greek (*Eikon Basilike*, supposedly written by King Charles I) and various biblical texts with references. The 'Royall Oake of Brittain' is being hacked and pulled down while its destroyer looks on and gives orders. Even the heavens themselves are ablaze, but who will also suffer when the tree falls? The whole cartoon is full of allegory and symbolism.

Compare this with the twentieth-century examples (Figures 5.6–5.8): how do these differ? Is it in style, caricature, symbolism, in verbal or visual content? What does each tell us as 'witting' or 'unwitting testimony' about the period in which it was drawn?

Lloyd George
and the double-
headed Ass

Figure 5.6

A NATION OF FIRE-EATERS.

Peaceful Teuton. "HIMMEL! THEY HAVE ALL THOSE ARMIES! AND THE FATHER-LAND HAS ONLY ONE!"

Figure 5.7

THEY SALUTE WITH BOTH HANDS NOW

Figure 5.8

Figure 5.9

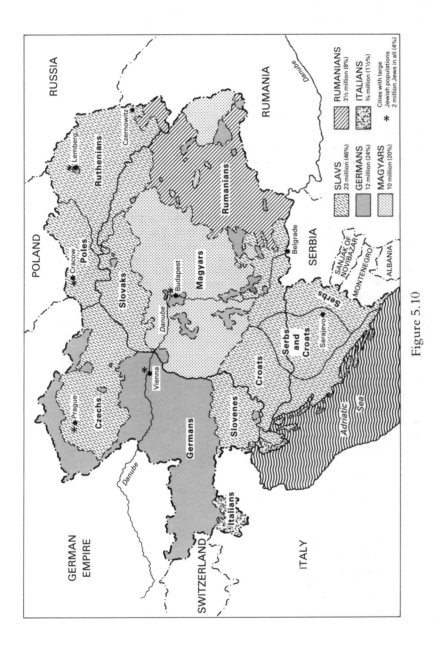

Figure 5.10

The map of the linguistic and ethnic nature of the Austro-Hungarian empire is an attempt to portray statistical evidence in the form of a map (Figure 5.10). What does it convey in cartography that the percentage figures by themselves do not?

Statistics

Statistics need *not* put historians off, though they sometimes do. A reasonably straightforward example (Figure 5.11) is the inventory of the possessions of John Bigg of Little Kimble, near Aylesbury, taken in 1703 (Buckinghamshire County Record Office). Once the 'Secretary hand' is identified – look at letters r, e, p, t, s and C – then all his personal, household and farming goods spring to life.

> The expenses of reparacons mayde aboutt the parish churche of Esingwold and the annornamentes of the same by Vmfraye Stavelay, Thomas Trewhytt, Thomas Leathlay and George Tewe, churchwardons of the same churche, sincce the entry of the Quenes majesty now being, that is to say the fyrst, secound, and thyrd yeare of hir reynge, to the whiche expenses the inhabitantes of Esingwolde do desyer to haue the inhabitauntes of Raskell to be contributors indifferenter cum dictis inhabitantibus de Esyngwolde

In Primis to a glasyer for mending the glass wyndoes	xs.	ijd.
Item to a plumber for mendinge the leades	iijs.	viijd.
Item a couering to the sacrament of thaulter		xxd.
Item to Lowrance Brice for mending the cloke	xs.	iiijd.
Item for a lytle messe booke prynted	ijs.	vjd.
Item to Robert Sharpp for mendyng the sepulcar		xvjd.
Item for ij bell bawtryes		xxijd.
Item for ij handbelles	ijs.	
Item for pullyes to the belles		iiijd.
Item for a holywattor cane		vd.
Item to Walshe for setting vppe the aulter		xijd.
Item for bynding of one booke	iijs.	viijd.
Item for wesshinge the church clothes	iijs.	iiijd.
Item to Ibson for making ij bell whelles	vjs.	viijd.
Item to John Walker for nales to the sayd whelles		vjd.
Item to George Carver for a nother bell whell	iijs.	iiijd.
Item for iij bellstringes	vs.	
Item for one anthyphonar	vjs.	viijd.
Item to Alane Gaytt for a royd with Mary and John	xvjs.	viijd.
Item for ij surplasses	xs.	iiijd.
Item to the glasyer for mending the glase wyndoes	xjs.	vd.
Item for ij busshelles of Lymee		viijd.
Item for vij pounde of leade		xiiijd.
Item for nales to the ploumber		vijd.
Item to Richard Leake wyff for wesshing of ij surplesses		iiijd.
Item to Robert Sharpp for mending the bell frame		vijd.
Item to Mr Fayrfax for a vestment	xjs.	
Item for irone to the clocke		xjd.

A True & perfect Inventory of all the goods & Chattell of John Bigg
of Little Kimboll in ye County of Bucks yeoman lately Deceased as they
wore taken & apprised ye 20 of September Anno Dom: 1703 by us
whose names are here under written ————— l s d

Sixteen Cows and a Bull ———————	050	0	0
Nine horses and a Colt —————	040	0	0
Two hundred thirty-to Sheep ———————	030	0	0
For Six hogs and to pigs —————	008	10	0
For: 46: Acres of wheat —	138	0	0
For 15: Acres of barly	030	0	0
For: 46: Acres of beans ———	063	0	0
For 10: Acres of oates ———	014	0	0
For 30: quarter of old beans ———	022	0	0
For ye hay ——————	025	0	0
For making the Silth	025	0	0
For all harness Collers ropes Saddle bridles ———	008	0	0
For ye wagon and Carts ———	015	0	0
For ye ploues harrows Donwraks & other implements belonging to	003	10	0
For ye Clock & things in ye hall ———————	002	15	0
For ye Table & Cares & other things in ye parler —	002	14	6
For ye pulter & brass & other things in ye Kithing —	007	4	6
For ye goods in ye dairy houf & ye Sollor	004	1	0
For ye goods in ye parler Chambor & bed & other things —	009		
For ye goods in ye hall Chambor & bed & other things —	005	12	0
For ye goods in ye Kithing Chambor & bed & other things —	006	4	0
For ye goods in ye next Chambor & to cestles & linnon —	014	4	0
For ye goods in ye in ye garrat Chambor bed & other things —	003	12	0
For ye Chees in ye Chees Chambor & boards & stands —	008	0	0
For ye goods in ye mens Chambor & bed & other lumber —	004	5	0
For ye Saks bushell Shovles & sives —	002	5	0
	547	16	6
For ye wearing apparell & money in his purse —	005	0	0
A Bond for a hundred pound ———	100	0	0
The Chattell which Cometh to ———	200	0	0
The whole Inventory Cometh to ———	852	16	6

Joseph Smith & Joseph Toydon

Inventory of the Goods of John Bigg of Little Kimble, Yeoman, lately deceased, 20 September 1703.

Figure 5.11

Item to Robert Clarke for mending the organs	iiij li.		
Item to John Walker for irone boundes to thorgans			xiijd.
Item for a manvell			xiijd.
Item to Walsh for mendinge the churche flewer			iiijd.
Item to Vmfray Stablerfora wesshing the church gear			viijd.
Summa	ix li.	xixs.	vd.

What do the parochial expenses at Easingwold, Yorkshire, suggest about the progress of the counter-reformation in Mary Tudor's reign? (from *The Reformation in the North to 1558* (ed.) W. J. Sheils, University of York, Borthwick Institute of Historical Research, 1976).

But caution is needed. Gregory King's famous population survey 'for the year 1688' has many pitfalls (from G. S. Holmes, 'Gregory King and the Social Structure of pre-industrial England', *Transactions of the Royal Historical Society*, 5th series, 27, 1977, 66–8). Apart from comprehension – for 'family' read 'household' – how did King obtain his information, was it reliable, did he write with a political or economic motive, what occupations were not listed (where *were* they?) and so on? The answers are, of course, quite complex, as the table was not merely designed as a piece of social inquiry.

The Peace Ballot of 1934–5 sets interpretative difficulties. Were the questions too simplistic, whereas no statesman operates outside a specific context? Did the answers suggest a pacifist spirit in Britain?

The Peace Ballot, July 1935

Question 3. Are you in favour of the all-round abolition of national military and naval aircraft by international agreement?

Total YES answers:	9,157,145
Total NO answers:	1,614,159
Percentage of YES answers in relation to total YES and NO answers:	85.0
Percentage of YES answers in relation to YES, NO and DOUBTFUL answers and ABSTENTIONS:	82.6

Question 5b. Do you consider that, if a nation insists on attacking another, the other nations should combine to compel it to stop by, if necessary, military measures?

Total YES answers:	6,506,777
Total NO answers:	2,262,261
Percentage of YES answers in relation to total YES and NO answers:	74.2
Percentage of YES answers in relation to total YES, NO, DOUBTFUL and CHRISTIAN PACIFIST answers and ABSTENTIONS:	58.6

APPENDIX

Gregory King's 'Scheme of the Income and Expense of the several Families of England, ... for the Year 1688'

(The 'Barnett version', 1936, from B. L. Harleian MS. 1898; amendments in square brackets from the revised, 'Davenant version', 1698[9])
N.B. The first five columns of figures and the last (9th) column only are reproduced below.
Column 7, 'Annual expenditure per family', has been reconstituted from King's per capita figures.

Number of Families	Ranks, Degrees, Titles, and Qualifications	Heads per Family	Number of Persons	Yearly Income per Family £	Total Yearly Income £	Annual Expenditure per Family £	Total Increase of Wealth Yearly £
160	Temporal Lords	40	6,400	2,800 [3,200]	448,000 [512,000]	2,400 [2,800]	64,000
26	Spiritual Lords	20	520	1,300	33,800	1,100 [900]	5,200 [10,400]
800	Baronets	16	12,800	880	704,000	816 [784]	51,200 [76,800]
600	Knights	13	13,800	650	390,000	598 [585]	31,200 [39,000]
3,000	Esquires	10	30,000	450	1,200,000	420 [410]	90,000 [120,000]
12,000	Gentlemen	8	96,000	280	2,880,000	260 [256]	240,000 [288,000]
5,000	Persons in [greater] offices [and places]	8	40,000	240	1,200,000	216 [208]	120,000 [160,000]
5,000	Persons in [lesser] offices [and places]	6	30,000	120	600,000	108 [102]	60,000 [90,000]
2,000	[Eminent] Merchants and Traders by Sea	8	16,000	400	800,000	320 [296]	160,000 [208,000]
8,000	[Lesser] Merchants and Traders by Sea	6	48,000	200 [198]	1,600,000 [1,584,000]*	168 [162]	240,000 [288,000]
10,000	Persons in the Law	7	70,000	140 [154]	1,400,000 [1,540,000]	119 [91]	210,000 [280,000]

Number of Families	Ranks, Degrees, Titles, and Qualifications	Heads per Family	Number of Persons	Yearly Income per Family £	Total Yearly Income £	Annual Expenditure per Family £	Total Increase of Wealth Yearly £
2,000	[Eminent] Clergymen	6	12,000	60 [72]	120,000 [144,000]	54 [60]	12,000 [24,000]
8,000	[Lesser] Clergymen	5	40,000	45 [50]	360,000 [400,000]	40 [47]	40,000 [32,000]
40,000	Freeholders [of the better sort]	7	280,000	84 [91]	3,360,000 [3,640,000]	77 [82–5]	280,000 [350,000]
140,000 [120,000]	Freeholders [of the lesser sort]	5 [5½]	700,000 [660,000]	50 [55]	7,000,000 [6,600,000]	47–10	350,000 [330,000]
150,000	Farmers	5	750,000	44 [42–10]	6,600,000	42–10 [41–5]	187,000 [187,500]
16,000 [15,000]	Persons in Sciences and Liberal Arts	5	80,000 [75,000]	60	960,000 [900,000]	57–10 [55]	40,000 [75,000]
40,000 [50,000]	Shopkeepers and Tradesmen	4½	180,000 [225,000]	45	1,800,000 [2,250,000]	42–15 [40–10]	90,000 [225,000]
60,000	Artisans and Handicrafts	4	240,000	40 [38]	2,400,000 [2,280,000]	38 [36]	120,000
5,000	Naval Officers	4	20,000	80	400,000	72	40,000
4,000	Military Officers	4	16,000	60	240,000	56	16,000
511,586 [500,586]		5¼ [5½]	2,675,520 [2,675,520]	67 [68–18]	34,495,800 [34,488,800]	63 [62–15]	2,447,100 [3,023,700]

*This *should* be the revised figure. In fact it stays as 1,600,00

Number of Families	Ranks, Degrees, Titles, and Qualifications	Heads per Family	Number of Persons	Yearly Income per Family £	Total Yearly Income £	Annual Expenditure per Family £	Total Increase of Wealth Yearly £
50,000	Common Seamen	3	150,000	20	1,000,000	22–10	Decrease 75,000
364,000	Labouring People and Outservants	3½	1,275,000	15	5,460,000	16–2	127,500
400,000	Cottagers and Paupers	3¼	1,300,000	6–10	2,000,000	7–6–3	325,000
35,000	Common Soldiers	2	70,000	14	490,000	15	35,000
849,000		3¼	2,795,000	10–10	8,950,000	11–4–3	562,500
	Vagrants as Gipsies, Thieves, Beggars, etc.		30,000	2	60,000	3	60,000
	So the General Account is				—	—	
511,586 [500,586]	Increasing the Wealth of the Kingdom	5¼ [5½]	2,675,520	67 [68–18]	34,495,800 [34,488,800]	63 [62–15]	2,447,100 [3,023,700]
849,000	Decreasing the Wealth of the Kingdom	3¼	2,825,000	10–10	9,101,000	10–19–4	622,500
1,360,586 [1,349,586]	NEAT TOTALS	4 1/20 [4 1/19]	5,500,520	32–0 [32–5]	43,505,800 [43,491,800]	30–12–7 [30–8–6]	1,825,100 [2,401,200]

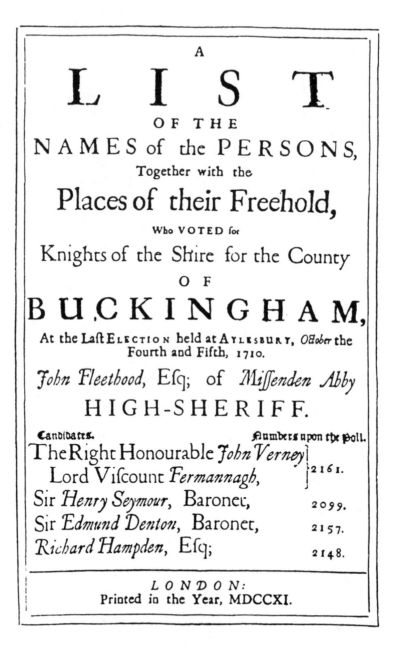

Figure 5.12

The extract from the 1710 Buckinghamshire county election pollbook (Figures 5.12 and 5.13) (Buckinghamshire County Record Office) also sets problems for the historian. Why did many freeholders with land in Steeple Claydon split their votes, when almost every voter in other villages either voted for the two Whigs – D[enton] and H[ampden] – or the two Tories – F[ermanagh] and S[eymour]? Why were some communities more Whig than Tory or *vice versa*? How could we find the answers to those questions?

Election statistics of a more general nature are given in *Twentieth Century Britain*, R. J. Brown and C. W. Daniels (1982) pp. 41–4, and questions offer advice on using this material to draw out significant points on the decline of the Liberal Party.

As Clive Trebilcock wrote, 'the key point is to realize that statistics possess no special life of their own; they are, in the vast majority of cases, illustrative of an argument that can be, and usually is, rendered in other ways . . . the student should approach the results themselves with a critical and creative judgement.' With that thought in mind, perhaps even the 'number-crunching' computer can be used with confidence. Nineteenth-century census information has been computerised to allow speedy comparisons within and between communities – age distribution, size of families, occupations, and so on – and *Nineteenth Century Britain*, R. J. Brown and C. W. Daniels (1980), pp. 33–8, included extracts from the 1851 census of Bury St Edmunds, Suffolk, relating to the Thingoe Union Workhouse. John Mills' computer program offers census information in a different form. What does it reveal about Thornborough, Buckinghamshire, in 1851, and what problems are there for the historian in the methods and results?

Column 1

Jofhua Geary	F	S
Elias Cock	F	S
Samuel Ware	F	S
William Gillet	F	S
Charles Phillips	F	S
William Seabrooke	F	S
Robert Wright	F	S
Thomas Ayres	F	S
Selvefter Byrd	F	S
Daniel Wyre	F	S
Thomas Stroughret	F	S
Mirke Morris	F	S
John Fryer	F	S
James Uwen	F	S
Richard Fryer	F	S
William Hill, Arm.	F	S
Francis King	F	S
Edward Waverfon	F	S
Thomas Nealer	F	S
William Tochfield	F	S
James Prefton	F	S
Thomas Brickwed	S	H
Robert l'Oncy	S	H
Thomas Fryer	S	H
William Childe, Arm.	D	H
John Horwood	D	H
William Chafe	D	H
John Chafe	D	H
Henry Lawrence	D	H
William Portus	D	H
John Catline	D	H
Richard Browne	D	H
John Prede	D	H
Daniel Pope	D	H
John White	D	H
William Brown	D	H
Jofiah Groove	D	H
Thomas Mann, Sen.	D	H
Thomas Mann, Jun.	D	H
John Fellowes	D	H
Robert Pratt	D	H
John Burch	D	H
John Benham	D	H
John Plaxer	D	H
Francis Prefd	D	H
Robert Caplyn	D	H
Richard Almond	D	H
Ralph Serjabourne	D	H
Nathaniel Cock	D	H
Richard Harding	D	H
Bernard Richardfon	D	H
James Atkinfon	D	H
Jofhua Look	D	H
Jacob Duval	D	H
Jofeph Dudd	D	H
Luke Leader	D	H
James Childe	D	H
Robert Pratt, Sr	D	H
John Fellow, Jun.	D	H
Philip Ware	D	H
Tymothy Betterfmill	D	H
John Dell	D	H
George Grocim	D	H
John Norwood	D	H
William Hill	D	H
Abraham Gray	D	H
John Coney	D	H
Thomas Bignal	D	H
Thomas Garraway	D	H
Samuel Jones	D	H
John Penne	D	H
Thomas Cock	D	H
Jofeph Salter	D	H
Richard Harris	D	H
Edward Kitfon	D	H
William Fellow	D	H
Nicholas Statham	D	H

Column 2

James Durrant	D	H
John Wilkinfon	D	H
John Wilkinfon, Jun.	D	H
Samuel Wooden	D	H
John Wingrave	D	H
William Weft	D	H
Henry Trumper	D	H
John Fincher	D	H
Jofeph Gurney	D	H
John Weatherhead	D	H
Daniel Batchelor	D	H
Henry Portenham	D	H
William Dearmer	D	H
William Lee	D	H
James Coleman	D	H
Thomas Parrat	D	H
Timothy Bampton	D	H
John Portenham	D	H
Richard Puttenham	D	H
James Harding	D	H
Nicholas Horwood	D	H
John Dell	D	H
Samuel Burch	D	H
Alexander Ayres	D	H
Edward Johnfon	D	H
William Parrot	D	H
Jofeph Potter	D	H
Thomas Emerton, Gent.	D	H
Daniel Switzer	D	H
Thomas Wordail	D	H
John Gotham	D	H
James Atkinfon	D	H
Thomas Parrat	D	H
John Delamore	D	H
Axiel Roberts, Afbridge	D	H
Charles Scorsby	D	H
Sebaftian Grace	D	H
John Ware	D	H
William Partridge	D	H
Jofeph Cock	D	H
Richard Barnes	D	H
Nathaniel Byrch	D	H
John Coleman	D	H
Daniel Roberts	D	H
Robert Aldridge	D	H
Robert Whitmore	D	H
James Worral	D	H
Samuel Sundford	D	H
John Prefton	D	H
Thomas Beder	—	H
John Puttenham	D	H
Francis Puttenham	D	H

3 Chefbam.

William Drake, Efq;	F	S
Henry Addington	F	—
John King	D	H
Richard Wadham	D	H
Richard Wadham, Jun.	D	H
William Ward	D	H

Chepues.

Charles Reed	D	H
Jofeph Hoz	D	H

Chicheley.

Sir John Chefter, Bart.	F	S
William Barber, Cl.	F	S
William Samms	F	S

Chilton.

Edward Harvey, Efq;	F	S
Robert Hart, Efq;	F	S
William Norchine, Efq;	F	S
John Saunders	F	S
Arthur Scholey	F	S
Richard Kinn	D	H

Column 3

Chowlesbury.

John Eyres	F	S

Cat Clapbon cum Bott Clepbon.

Peter Duncombe, Gent.	F	S
Prefton Duncombe, Gent.	F	S
Oliver Worthington, Gent.	F	S
John Lee	F	S
Thomas Harding	F	S
John Kodwel	F	S
Thomas Millward	F	D
William Wilfon	F	D
William Abell, Efq;	D	H
Richard Abell	D	H
Francis Green, Cl.	D	H
William Tame	D	H
Thomas Miller	D	H
Thomas Holland	D	H
John Edlin	D	H
Nathaniel Holland	D	—
Thomas Smith	D	H
John Smith, Bart.	D	H

Middle Clapbon.

John Lord Vifcount Fermanagh	S	—
The Honourable Ralph Verney	F	S
William Buncfhill, Cl.	F	S

Steeple Clapbon.

William Challoner, Gent.	F	S
Edward Challoner, Gent.	F	S
James Challoner, Gent.	F	S
Charles Challoner, Gent.	F	S
John Robinfon	F	S
Richard Petifer	F	S
William Hapbey	F	S
Thomas Blake	F	S
Robert Flexman	F	S
Edward Birton	F	S
Thomas Brace	F	S
Nicholas Wallis	F	S
Richard Irons	F	S
Edward Taylor	F	S
Thomas Robinfon	F	S
Francis Eyres	F	S
Richard Abbot	F	S
James Dobfon, Gent.	F	S
William Birton	F	D
Thomas Abbot	F	D
Benjamin Bates	F	—
Henry Wootton	F	D
Thomas Grimes	F	D
Richard Cox	F	D
Edmund Bradbury	F	D
James Cox	F	D
John Inns	F	D
John Reeve	F	D
Thomas Snow	F	D
William Hofle	F	D
Henry Triplett	F	D
Richard Triplett	F	D
John Triplett	F	D
Thomas King	F	D
Edward Ingram	F	D
Michael Millar	D	H
James Butts	D	H
John Dereul	D	H
John Juckfn	D	H
John Wark	D	H
Mich. Anderfon	D	H
William Norman	D	H
Samuel Norman	D	H
Jofeph Churchil	D	H

Clifton

Figure 5.13

Clifton Reynes.

Thomas Page — F S
Richard Pedley — D H

Colnbrook.

Isaac Torton — F S
Richard Wakefield — F S
John Gay — F S
Thomas Gay — F S
William Reynolds — F S
Thomas Beddale — F S
John Thompson — F S
Thomas Reyner —
John Barcombe — D H
Thomas Reynolds — D H
William West — D H
William Goodpit — D H
William Dean — D H
John Cooke — D H
John Childe — D H
Ralph Scudd — D H

North Crawley.

Thomas Dewberry, Cl. — F S
Robert Cowley — F S
Edward Cowley — F S
Joseph Greenwood — F S
John Hall — F S
Edward Burge — F S
George Burge — F S
Edward Kingham — F S
John Lamley — F S
Thomas Hall — F S
George Flexn — F S
Robert North — F S
Robert Hall — F S
Gilbert Pickering — F S
Edmund Shorthorpe — F S
William Williamson — F S
William Smallbones — F S
Thomas Harding — F S
John Boucher — F S
Isaac Busby — F S
Thomas Page — F S
Thomas Barret — F S
Thomas Fellows — F S
John Glidewell — F S
John Brinton — F S
John Kidcby — F S
Richard Hall — F S
William Levens — F S
Robert Austin — F S
Benjamin Beal — F S
Thomas Nash — F S
Thomas Nottingham — F S
John Vaux — F S
John Hoskins — F S
John Markes — F S
William Arpin — F S
George Sheppard — F S
Bernard Franks, Asr. — D H
Robert Church — D H
John Tyndley — D H
William Forster — D H
Edward Dynn — D H
John Forscot — D H
Edward Dynn — D M

Long Crendon.

William Clarke, Cl. — F S
William Cannon, Gent. — F S

William Cannon, Jun. — F S
John Randal — F S
John Baker — F S
Edward Nicholls — F S
Robert Beck — F S
John Baker, Jun. — F S
William Grace — F S
Edward Randal — F S
William Neighbour — F S
John Willis — F S
James Perry — F S
Francis Wallis — F S
John Towersey — F S
Henry Reynolds — F S
John Towersey, Jun. — F S
William Thompson —
Thomas Heath — F S
Edward Thompson — F S
Thomas Wisser — F S
John Lucas — F S
Richard Goodwyn — F S
Thomas Towersey — F S
Peter Neighbour — D H
John Rider — D H
William Allen — D H
Henry Symms — D H
John Cotterell — D H
William Parker — D H
John Nicholls — D H
Peter Neighbour — D H
Richard Herne — D H
John Carfoot — D H
Joseph Cock — D H
Nicholas Towersey — D H
Thomas Greening — D H
Richard Symson — D H
John Beringer — D H
Thomas Newtons — D M
Henry West — D H
John Hester — D M
Edward bridge — D M
William Wyatt — D H
Thomas Grace — D H
William Green — D H
Thomas Reynolds — D H
William Cocks — D H
Thomas Howlet — D M
Thomas Cox — D M

Cublington.

Francis Cooley, Asr. — F S
William Heady — F S
Thomas Keen — F S
Robert Barnary — F S
Thomas Hedges — F S
Richard Coles — F S
Richard Keen — F S
Thomas Harris — F S
John Keen — F S
Richard Golther — F S
Thomas Wagstaff, Cl. — F H
Robert Coles — F H
Samuel Goodman — D H
George Snone — D H
William Green — D H
Richard Worral — D H
William Gence — D H
Thomas Gower — D H
George Coles — D H
Isaac Green — D M
John Bellington — D H
Robert Fletcher — D H
John Grace — D H
John Lucas — D H
William King — D H

George Apsley — D H
John Riccott — D H
William Symson, Sen. — D H

Chicheley.

William Veary — F S
Thomas Piddington — F S
John Greenwood — F S
George Hopper — F S
William Dixon — F S
John Playstead — F S
Thomas Moores — F S
Thomas Sommer, Esq. — D H
John Cox — D H
James Pidington — D H
John Baron — D H
William Beach — D H
Francis Goddard — D H
William Lamborne — D H
William Guildford — D H
Ephraim Holt — D H
Richard Baker — D H
Thomas Veery — D H
Benjamin Eastace — D H
Henry Clracoe — D H
Richard Slaughter — D H
John Vaux — D H
Paul Hows, pr. Symss. — D H
Thomas Burymourne — D H
Charles Fynd — D H
Jos. Role — D H
William Barnard — D H

Datchett.

Benjamin Lane, Esq. — F S
Henry Tothill, Gent. — F S
John Seymour — F S
Henry Temple — F S
William Barrington — F S
John Warren — F S
William Herbert — F S
John Meate — F S
William Hale — F S
Edward Dearl — F S
Joseph Callwey — D H

Drayton.

Cecil Bowyer, Esq. — F S
Thomas Carter, Gent. — F S
Thomas Carter, Jun. Gent. — F S
Richard Kedge — F S
Thomas Glmerest — F S
John Glmerest — F S
William Gilbert — F S
Edmund Beezle — F S
James Gale — F S
Thomas Grge — F S
John Gladares — F S
Richard Price — F S
John Berusham — F S
Edward Long — F S
John Hill — F S
Sir Roger Hill, Kt. — D H
Roger Hill, Esq. — D H
Francis Knight — D H
Robert Tyler — D H
Thomas Weedon, Gent. — D H
Thomas Kees — D H
Robert Jukemas — D H
Thomas Hale — D H
John Symson — D H
Thomas Holland — D H
Christopher Gotham — Edmund

C

Figure 5.13 (continued)

MILLS HISTORICAL AND COMPUTING Survey of Rural Victorian Communities Thornborough, Bucks, 1851

Total enumerated resident population: 752

	No.	%
Males:	379	50.4
Females:	373	49.6

Marital Status	No.	%		%		%
Unmarried:	413	54.9	M = 210	55.4	F = 203	54.4
Married:	291	38.7	M = 147	38.8	F = 144	38.6
Widowed:	48	6.4	M = 22	5.8	F = 26	7

Household size by no. of persons	1	2	3	4	5	6	7	8	9	10
No. of households	9	43	39	38	21	13	9	10	3	3
No. of persons	9	86	117	152	105	78	63	80	27	30

Household size by no. of persons	11	12	13	14	15	16	17	18	19	20
No. of households	0	0	0	0	0	0	0	0	0	0
No. of persons	0	0	0	0	0	0	0	0	0	0

Mean household size = 4 persons   Number of Households: 188

Birthplaces
(Local = within 5 mls   Distant = beyond 5 mls)

	No.	%	Male N	Male %	Female N	Female %
Natives	501	66.6	289	57.7	212	42.3
Outsiders	251	33.4	90	35.9	161	64.1
Local	105	41.8	34	32.4	71	67.6
Distant	146	58.2	56	38.4	90	61.6

Males	No.	% of M	Unmarried N	Unmarried %	Married N	Married %	Widowed N	Widowed %
Natives	289	76.3	174	60.2	103	35.6	12	4.2
Outsiders	90	23.7	36	40	44	48.9	10	11.1
Local	34		10	29.4	21	61.8	3	8.8
Distant	56		26	46.4	23	41.1	7	12.5

Females	No.	% of F	Unmarried N	Unmarried %	Married N	Married %	Widowed N	Widowed %
Natives	212	56.8	153	72.2	51	24.1	8	3.8
Outsiders	161	43.2	50	31.1	93	57.8	18	11.2
Local	71		16	22.5	48	67.6	7	9.9
Distant	90		34	37.8	45	50	11	12.2

Number of persons with no recorded birthplace = 0

	No.	%	Males	%	Females	%
FM Farmers and similar	20	5.9	20	100	0	0
FW Farm workers and similar	164	48.7	161	98.2	3	1.8
TCM Traders/craftsmen, masters	16	4.7	16	100	0	0
TCJ Traders, journeymen, other employees	10	3	9	90	1	10
TC Traders, undifferentiated	70	20.8	28	40	42	60
FAC Factory workers	10	3	10	100	0	0
PEG Professional, large entrepreneurs, gents	10	3	5	50	5	50
SER Servants	29	8.6	1	3.4	28	96.6
X Special occupation of the locality	0	0	0	0	0	0
Z All others employed	8	2.4	7	87.5	1	12.5
Totals	337	100	257		80	

Total classified = 337 = 44.8% of population
Residual = 415 = 55.2% of population
Total population = 752

				Males			Females		
	Native	Local	Distant	Native	Local	Distant	Native	Local	Distant
FM	9	2	9	9	2	9	0	0	0
%	45	10	45	45	10	45	0	0	0
FW	133	11	20	131	11	19	2	0	1
%	81.1	6.7	12.2	81.4	6.8	11.8	66.7	0	33.3
TCM	9	4	3	9	4	3	0	0	0
%	56.3	25	18.8	56.3	25	18.8	0	0	0
TCJ	5	3	2	4	3	2	1	0	0
%	50	30	20	44.4	33.3	22.2	100	0	0
TC	54	8	8	19	3	6	35	5	2
%	77.1	11.4	11.4	67.9	10.7	21.4	83.3	11.9	4.8
FAC	9	0	1	9	0	1	0	0	0
%	90	0	10	90	0	10	0	0	0
PEG	2	3	5	1	2	2	1	1	3
%	20	30	50	20	40	40	20	20	60
SER	6	7	16	0	0	1	6	7	15
%	20.7	24.1	55.2	0	0	100	21.4	25	53.6
X	0	0	0	0	0	0	0	0	0
%	0	0	0	0	0	0	0	0	0
Z	2	1	5	2	1	4	0	0	1
%	25	12.5	62.5	28.6	14.3	57.1	0	0	100
—	272	66	76	105	8	9	167	58	67
%	65.7	15.9	18.4	86.1	6.6	7.4	57.2	19.9	22.9

OTHER NOTES: FAC = Coombs brickyard

Age Bands	Total No.	%	Numbers Nat	Loc	Dist	All Males	Percentages of total population Males Nat	Loc	Dist	All Females Fems	Nat	Loc	Dist
80+	5	0.7	1	2	2	0.5	0.1	0.1	0.3	0.1	0	0.1	0
75–79	7	0.9	2	2	3	0.3	0.1	0	0.1	0.7	0.1	0.3	0.3
70–74	14	1.9	5	4	5	0.7	0.4	0.1	0.1	1.2	0.3	0.4	0.5
65–69	17	2.3	14	2	1	1.3	1.2	0.1	0	0.9	0.7	0.1	0.1
60–64	19	2.5	7	6	6	1.2	0.7	0.4	0.1	1.3	0.3	0.4	0.7
55–59	29	3.9	15	4	10	2.4	1.7	0.3	0.4	1.5	0.3	0.3	0.9
50–54	41	5.5	21	8	12	2.5	1.7	0.3	0.5	2.9	1.1	0.8	1.1
45–49	39	5.2	25	6	8	2.3	1.7	0.1	0.4	2.9	1.6	0.7	0.7
40–44	36	4.8	21	7	8	2.7	2	0.3	0.4	2.1	0.8	0.7	0.7
35–39	38	5.1	21	7	10	2	1.3	0.4	0.3	3.1	1.5	0.5	1.1
30–34	30	4	10	9	11	2.1	1.1	0.4	0.7	1.9	0.3	0.8	0.8
25–29	67	8.9	34	15	18	4.9	3.2	0.5	1.2	4	1.3	1.5	1.2
20–24	73	9.7	42	13	18	5.3	3.5	0.5	1.3	4.4	2.1	1.2	1.1
15–19	85	11.3	59	9	17	5.7	4.7	0.3	0.8	5.6	3.2	0.9	1.5
10–14	67	8.9	56	2	9	3.6	3.2	0	0.4	5.3	4.3	0.3	0.8
5–9	83	11	72	8	3	5.5	4.8	0.5	0.1	5.6	4.8	0.5	0.3
0–4	102	13.6	96	1	5	7.4	7	0.1	0.3	6.1	5.7	0	0.4

Number of persons with no recorded age = 0
See the first sheet for unrecorded birthplaces

Key: 0 = Natives   + = Local   : = Distant

	Males		Females
80+		:	
75–79		+:	
70–74	00	0++::	
65–69	000000	000	
60–64	++000	0++:::	
55–59	::+00000000	0+:::::	
50–54	::+00000000	00000+++::::::	
45–49	::00000000	00000000+++:::	
40–44	::+0000000000	0000+++:::	
35–39	:++000000	0000000++::::::	
30–34	:::++00000	0++++::::	
25–29	::::::++000000000000000	000000+++++++::::::	
20–24	:::::::++0000000000000000	0000000000+++++++:::::	
15–19	:::::+0000000000000000000000	0000000000000000++++:::::::	
10–14	::00000000000000000	000000000000000000000+::::	
5–9	++00000000000000000000000	00000000000000000000000++:	
0–4	OFF SCALE, Refer to figures above	0000000000000000000000000000::	

7% 6% 5% 4% 3% 2% 1%   0   1% 2% 3% 4% 5% 6% 7%

Oral Evidence

Oral evidence is increasingly used for reminiscences and 'first hand' evidence. Paul Thompson, in *The Voice of the Past*, wrote that 'oral history gives history back to the people *in their own words*. . . . It thrusts life into history itself and widens its scope. It allows heroes not just from the leaders but from the unknown majority of the people.' But this does not exempt oral evidence from the normal scrutiny given to other categories of evidence. *Old Men Forget* was the title of one politician's autobiography, but 'old men' can also distort by accident or design. Yet the best of these records have an immediacy and a vivid quality that evokes an episode superbly. The following examples are from contemporary accounts of the Western Front in the First World War, the first by an author and poet, the second from a more 'ordinary' viewpoint:

(a) Edmund Blunden

It was now approaching the beginning of November, and the days were melancholy and the colour of clay. We took over that deathtrap known as the Schwaben Redoubt, the way to which lay through the fallen fortress of Thiepval. One had heard the worst accounts of the place, and they were true. Crossing the Ancre again at Black Horse Bridge, one went up through the scanty skeleton houses of Authuille, and climbing the dirty little road over the steep bank, one immediately entered the land of despair. Bodies, bodies and their useless gear heaped the gross waste ground; the slimy road was soon only a mud track which passed a whitish tumulus of ruin with lurking entrances, some spikes that had been pinetrees, a bricked cellar or two, and died out. The village pond, so blue on the map, had completely disappeared. The Ligne de Pommiers had been grubbed up. The shell-holes were mostly small lakes of what was no doubt merely rusty water, but had a red and foul semblance of blood. Paths glistened weakly from tenable point to point. Of the dead, one was conspicuous. He was a Scottish soldier, and was kneeling, facing east, so that one could scarcely credit death in him; he was seen at some little distance from the usual tracks, and no one had much time in Thiepval just then for sight-seeing, or burying. Death could not kneel so, I thought, and approaching I ascertained with a sudden shrivelling of spirit that Death could and did.

Beyond the area called Thiepval on the map a trench called St. Martin's Lane led forward; unhappy he who got into it! It was blasted out by intense bombardment into a broad shapeless gorge, and pools of mortar-like mud filled most of it. A few duckboards lay half submerged along the parapet, and these were perforce used by our companies, and calculatingly and fiercely shelled at moments by the enemy. The wooden track ended, and then the men fought their way on through the gluey morass, until not one nor two were reduced to tears and impotent wild cries to God. They were not yet at the worst of their duty, for the Schwaben Redoubt ahead was an almost obliterated cocoon of trenches in which mud, and death, and life were much the same thing – and there the deep dugouts, which faced the German guns, were cancerous with torn bodies, and to pass an entrance was to gulp poison; in one place a corpse had apparently been thrust in to stop up a doorway's dangerous displacement, and an arm swung stupidly. Men of the next battalion were found in mud up to the armpits, and their fate was not spoken of; those who found them could not get them out. The whole zone was a corpse, and the mud itself mortified. Here we were to 'hold the line,' for an uncertain sentence of days.

(*Undertones of War*, E. Blunden, 1928, pp. 129–31)

(b) Sister Calder

In a camp hospital it's dirty because the ground is earth, there's no linoleum on the floor, nor wood. It was simply grass, we were walking on grass all the time – or rather it was grass before it turned into mud. And, of course, we were shelled and had shell-holes round about. It was that week at No. 19 that Matron fell into a shell-hole one night when she was doing a night round. We searched for her all over the place, because she was needed in the hospital and couldn't be found. Finally she was found dragging herself out of this shell-hole, a great deep one from one of those very heavy high-explosive shells. She'd been in it an hour and she'd just managed to prevent herself from being drowned, for it was full of water.

We'd had boys coming in all week, of course, and we'd been busy, but the ones we got at the weekend were in a shocking state, because so many of them had been lying out in the mud before they could be picked up by the first-aid orderlies. Their clothes were simply filthy. They didn't look like clothes at all. We had to cut them off and do what we could. But it was too late for a lot of them, and many a one lost an arm or a leg that would have healed up right away if he'd been brought straight in. We felt terribly sorry for them but we had to try not to show our feelings, because it would never have done. We'd all have been sunk in gloom and then we'd have been no good to the men. But it was difficult when a man was very badly wounded, wounded in a very difficult place perhaps. It was hard not to show sympathy.

(Sister J. Calder, No. 19 Casualty Clearing Station at Remy Siding, in *They Called it Passchendaele*, L. Macdonald, 1978, pp. 126–7)

Some institutions such as the Imperial War Museum are collecting memories and storing them on tapes which may be loaned, or consulted as transcripts.

Margaret Bowker wrote that 'a reverence towards complexity, tempered by imagination and insight, and controlled always by the nature of the evidence, are important attitudes to learn in evaluating the situations in which men [and women!] found themselves involved many centuries ago and in comprehending the thoughts which determined their actions.' Imagination and insight can certainly be developed by studying the varieties of evidence other than written or printed. Only a small selection of topics has been illustrated in this chapter, but what visual, statistical or oral material could be used for:

(a) the Welfare State in Britain since 1948;
(b) the Hungarian uprising of 1956;
(c) the Court of Louis XIV;
(d) eighteenth-century landscape gardens;
(e) nineteenth-century Union Workhouses;
(f) the English Civil Wars?

A Vital Map?

In connection with the last topic, the plan of Marston Moor (Figure 5.14), and a comment on its value, highlights some of the difficulties associated with assessing the value of visual evidence. The plan was prepared by the Royalist engineer Sir Bernard de Gomme, and shows the disposition of the Royalist, Parliamentary and Scotch armies at the battle of Marson Moor, 2 July 1644. But is it all that it seems, and will it stand the emphasis that some military historians have placed upon it?

Sir Bernard de Gomme's Plan of the Battle

Consideration of this sketch plan of the royalist forces at the start of the battle . . . is an indication of the importance that has been attached to it. Most recently, Brigadier Young emphasised its significance, and praised de Gomme as 'rather a good surveyor', a judgement which he arrived at from the single similarity of the line of a hedge drawn on de Gomme's plan, to the line of a ditch shown on the 6″ Ordnance Survey map of the area. Yet this similarity ought to be called in question, if for no other reason than that it appears to be the only accurate aspect of the entire plan. De Gomme drew up an order of battle for the royalist army which Young admits may not have prevailed on the field, because of the late arrival of the York Foot Regiments under General James King. At the best, it must be supposed that de Gomme's plan was probably a proposal rather than a subsequent depiction of reality. It shows bodies of horse and foot in battle order north of a hedge: it makes no attempt to show computed distances either between bodies or between the hedge and the army. Nor does it show any features of the terrain beyond the ridge line to the south. Most importantly, however, there is an omission from the list of royalist brigades. There is evidence that Colonel Sir John Mayney, of Linton in Kent, who was acting as brigade commander after Marston Moor, actually commanded a brigade in the battle. Mayney is missing from de Gomme's plan.

Above the ridge line, which de Gomme shows, the Scottish and Parliamentary army is sketched in without any attempt at distinguishing divisions. The sketch is intended to be purely representational, with a rough estimate of their numbers added. From the plan, it cannot be deduced whether the allied army was on top of, behind, or on both sides, of the ridge summit, a lack of accuracy akin to that evident in treatment of the royalist dispositions.

Between the ridge line and the hedge, de Gomme wrote 'A Descending Ground from the hill, to the hedge'. Simply, this is not true. . . . There are two ridge lines, an upper and a lower. Infantry advancing from the upper would go steeply downhill, march into a shallow, and then march uphill again, before reaching a level and descending slowly on to the moor proper. Either de Gomme could not observe this, or he did not care to note it . . . it . . . lends weight to the proposition that de Gomme's plan is almost certainly no more than a sketch, drawn up probably at Rupert's command, for the better marshalling of his army. No other importance can otherwise be attached to it.

Firth . . . believed that de Gomme drew up the plan after the battle, perhaps from an original and more hasty sketch. This is a reasonable conjecture, in view of the painstaking care which went into naming and colouring the formations: but it is strange, that this care, if de Gomme were indeed 'a good surveyor', was not extended to the rest of the moor and the terrain even in minor ways, such as noting tracks and

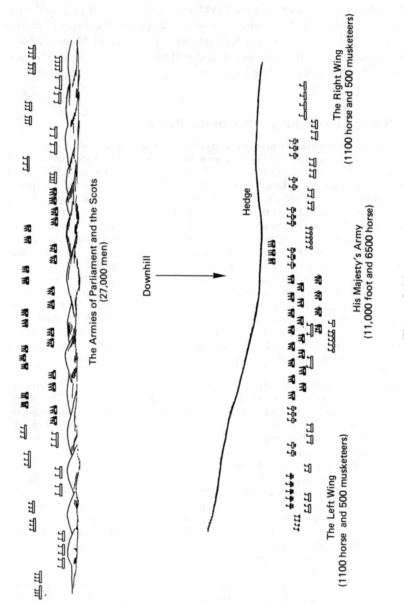

The Armies of Parliament and the Scots
(27,000 men)

Downhill

Hedge

The Right Wing
(1100 horse and 500 musketeers)

His Majesty's Army
(11,000 foot and 6500 horse)

The Left Wing
(1100 horse and 500 musketeers)

Figure 5.14

obstacles, more so if he managed the revision at his leisure as Firth suggests. It is quite possible that de Gomme used his original plan for subsequent elaboration, for there is no evidence that he ever drew it up for later historians, like Clarendon. This is demonstrated by the very point to which Firth drew attention, that is, the hypothetical plans for the battle drawn up by later writers who pieced their dispositions together from miscellaneous tracts and letters and memoirs which, when compared to de Gomme's plan, show a good deal of error. The absence of Mayney is a case in point. One eminently competent local historian, although writing when de Gomme's plan was well known, dismissed it as valueless. All in all, it is quite probable that de Gomme drew in the hedge line merely to indicate the existence of some barrier between the armies, without any considerations of accuracy. The value of the plan lies firstly in its contemporary origin, and secondly in its notation of regiments and commanders (not necessarily, of their dispositions). It must be treated with extreme caution in determining the course of the battle.

(*Marston Moor, 2 July 1644: The Sources and the Site*, P. R. Newman, Borthwick Papers No. 53, University of York Borthwick Institute of Historical Research, 1978, pp. 3–5)

6 Secondary Sources

'To expect a man to retain everything he has ever read is like expecting him to carry about in his body everything that he has ever eaten'
(Schopenhauer, *On Reading and Books*)

How many times have you been accused of failing to 'read round the subject'? How often have you been faced with having to read what seems to you a massive volume? How should you approach this task? This chapter is concerned with the nature of secondary sources and the ways in which you can approach them successfully and efficiently.

The Historian's Technique

Secondary sources – books, essays, articles – are works produced by historians based upon primary sources as well as a consideration of what other historians have said. The three basic techniques used by historians are description, narration and interpretation and these are combined in different ways. Books written by historians are *not* just collections of 'facts', although one of the most important functions of historians is the responsibility for presenting those 'facts' as clearly and accurately as possible. There is a tension between presenting the 'facts' and the necessity to interpret them. It is the historian who offers an explanation and interpretation of how the relevant facts are related to each other. How and why things happened are logical extensions of asking what happened. The 'facts' cannot speak for themselves but only through the historian's interpretations. Historians rewrite the past because there are generally alternative explanations, unexplored avenues, new techniques which make re-examination of the primary evidence both worthwhile and necessary. Perspectives change, societies develop. History is, in the words of Peter Geyl, 'an argument without end'.

Description and Narration

Historians attempt to recreate the historical moment as fully as possible. Description plays a valuable part in this process by attempting to create an empathy between the reader and the past. This requires literary skills as much as, perhaps more than, historical ones. Knowing the sources may not be enough. Imagination, feeling and creativity are skills more readily associated with the poet or dramatist. There are few historians who are artists in that sense. Guicciardini, Voltaire, Gibbon, Carlyle and Macaulay were all masters of historical description.

The declining health and last illness of Severus inflamed the wild ambition and black passions of Caracalla's soul. Impatient of any delay or division of empire, he attempted, more than once, to shorten the small remainder of his father's days, and endeavoured, but without success, to excite a mutiny among the troops. The old emperor had often censured the misguided lenity of Marcus (Aurelius) who, by a single act of justice, might have saved the Romans from the tyranny of his son (Commodus). Placed in the same situation, he experienced how easily the rigour of judge dissolves away in the tenderness of a parent. He deliberated, he threatened, but he could not punish; and this last and only instance of mercy was more fatal to the empire than a long series of cruelties. The disorder of his mind irritated the pains of his body; he wished impatiently for death, and hastened the instant of it by his own impatience.

(Edward Gibbon, *The Decline and Fall of the Roman Empire*, ed. N. M. Low, Penguin, 1963, p. 63)

As the clocks strike ten, behold the Place de la Révolution, once Place de Louis Quinze: the Guillotine, mounted near the old pedestal where once stood the Statue of that Louis! Far round, all bristles with cannons and armed men: spectators crowding in the rear; D'Orléans Egalité there in cabriolet. Swift messengers, hoguotons, speed to the Townhall, every three minutes; near by is the Convention sitting – vengeful for Lepelletier. Heedless of all, Louis reads his Prayers for the Dying; not till five minutes yet has he finished; then the carriage opens. What temper is he in? Ten different witnesses will give ten different accounts of it. He is in collision of all tempers; arrives now at the black Mahlstrom and descent of Death; in sorrow, in indignation struggling to be resigned. He mounts the scaffold, not without delay; he is in puce coat, breeches of gray, white stockings. He strips off his coat; stands disclosed in a sleeve-waistcoat of white flannel. The Executioners approach to bind him; he spurns, resists; Abbé Edgeworth has to remind him how the Saviour, in whom men trust, submitted to be bound. His hands are tied; the fatal moment has come. He advances towards the edge of the Scaffold, 'his face is red', and says: 'Frenchmen I die innocent: it is from the Scaffold and near approaching God that I tell you so. I pardon my enemies: I desire that France –' . . . The drums drown the voice. . . . The Executioners, desperate lest themselves be murdered, seize the hapless Louis: six of them desperate, him singly desperate, struggling there; bind him to their plank. Abbé Edgeworth, stooping, bespeaks him: 'Son of Saint Louis, ascend to Heaven.' The Axe clanks down; a King's life is shorn away. It is Monday the 21st of January 1793. He was aged Thirty-eight years four months and twenty-eight days.

(Thomas Carlyle, *The French Revolution*, printed in Thomas Carlyle, *Selected Essays*, Penguin 1971, pp. 146–7)

(1) Compare and contrast the styles used by Gibbon and Carlyle.
(2) How successful do you think each is in evoking the spirit of the past and why?
(3) Why should historians also be artists?

Historians are perhaps less 'literary' today than in the past. But some are still capable of producing evocative books: witness the work of Marc Bloch, especially his *Feudal Society*; Braudel's breathless perspective of the Mediterranean in the sixteenth century; Le Roy Ladurie's study of the peasants of Languedoc and his incisive and amusing *Montaillou*; E. P. Thompson's majestic and infuriating *The Making of the English Working Class*. Sometimes fictional accounts do more to recreate the past than more scholarly ones. Examples are Umberto Eco's novel *The Name of the Rose* which tells us much about the monastic life and its tensions in fourteenth-century Italy, and Graham Swift's *Waterland* with its picture of the Fens in the 1940s and the nature of the past.

It is through narrative that the main technique of the historian is seen. The origins of history lie in the story or tale. The boundary between the creative story and factual history has always been blurred – Homer's tales of Troy, Vergil's *Aeneid*, Beowulf, the Mabinogion, the Nordic sagas and the Arthurian legend all have a basis in the actual past. It is through narrative that historians express their major concern, the passage of time. The subjects of narratives vary – an account of a battle, a parliamentary session, a court case, a biography – but the ability to arouse emotions, create suspense and enter into the minds of historical actors does not.

Interpretation

Once historians begin to ask how and why they begin to explain and interpret the past. Both narrative and description require an explanatory framework of causation and consequence. How does the particular subject fit into the broader canvas of its contemporary world? What motivated individuals to act as they did? Explanation helps to restore that immediacy of experience. Explanations differ. Historians disagree. History requires different interpretations but not all interpretation is good history. One historian's opinion is not as good as another's if it is based upon poor research and bad presentation of argument.

Though some historians talk about 'revival of narrative' and others about 'scientific' history or historical sociology, description, narrative and explanation each still play an important part in any historical interpretation. Scientific and artistic qualities both need to be present in historians' work. The varied nature of evidence, of techniques employed and of historians themselves means that there will always be alternative interpretations, but the subject matter of history is varied. Lewis Namier wrote that:

> The subject matter of history is human affairs, men in action, things that have happened and how they happened; concrete events fixed in time and space, and their grounding in the thoughts and feelings of men – not things universal and generalised; events as complex and diversified as the men who wrought them . . .

whose ideas are but distantly related to reality and who are never moved by reason alone.

(1) Why are there so many different interpretations of past events?
(2) How can historians come to different conclusions from the same evidence?
(3) How do historians resolve the tension between the desire to recreate the past and the urge to interpret it?
(4) Changes in the social function of history have led to changes in the way historians have written about the past. Discuss.
(5) Historians need to be technical and imaginative, scientific and stylistic in their writings. Discuss.

Using Secondary Sources

So how should you use secondary sources? Reading is an active *not* a passive process. It requires time and energy but there are several useful techniques which allow you to maximise on your efforts.

First you need to be clear what *your purpose* is in reading a book or article. This influences any groundwork you do before you read. For example, you have been asked to prepare for a lesson on an unfamiliar topic. You have been given a couple of references to look through to try and identify the main points and issues. This requires one method of reading but for writing a detailed critique of an article different reading skills would be necessary. You will read material for different purposes and you will need to approach it in different ways.

Secondly you need to know whether the material *answers your needs*. You need to develop the ability to evaluate material quickly. This is essential if you are not to waste valuable time. Ask the following questions.

(1) Is the publication sufficiently up-to-date for your present needs? When was the book written? Which edition is the book? Has it been revised? Is the book a translation?
(2) Is it at the right level at this stage of your course? Is it too simple or difficult for you? Why?
(3) What is its scope? Is the table of contents sufficiently detailed to be helpful? What sections appear to be interesting, familiar or difficult to you? How do the contents relate to your purpose? What do the introduction and conclusion tell you about the book?
(4) Does it contain the information you need? What does an examination of the index add to your understanding of the content of the book? Does the index deal with ideas and concepts, people and places? Has the index sufficient detail to enable you easily to locate your areas of interest? How comprehensive are any footnotes, endnotes or a bibliography? Is there

any visual material, such as graphs, diagrams, tables, charts, maps, photographs and is it easy to follow?

(5) Is this book likely to be useful to you? If there are several books which you could use then which is likely to be of most use to you?

This process should certainly be applied to any material which you have found for yourself in the library. But it is still worthwhile looking at the anatomy of the book even if it has been recommended by your teacher.

Thirdly, although the 'facts' contained in the material are important they are often forgotten relatively soon after being learnt. In the long run it is more important to remember the author's interpretation of how the facts relate to each other and to understand the author's frame of reference.

It is usually possible to distinguish between the *subject* of a book and the *thesis* or interpretation being put forward by the author. It is important to identify the thesis early so that when you read the rest of the book you can examine its factual material against the central unifying argument. The more familiar you are with a subject the easier it is to concentrate critically on the interpretation. In doing this you will be thinking creatively, not just absorbing masses of information. It is useful to begin by reading the introductions and conclusions of books and articles since this is where the authors' interpretations are usually found. After you have established the thesis the rest of the material can be read quickly and efficiently.

Fourthly, you need to look at the author. Authors make many value judgements in their writing and it is important to identify their underlying assumptions and values. The following questions are worth asking:

(1) Does the book reflect an identifiable national, religious, political or ideological point of view? For example, British accounts of the American War of Independence differ from American ones and Russian views of Stalin from French ones.

(2) What is the emphasis of the author? Is the approach used a conscious decision? Because history is such a varied discipline there are many ways of approaching any subject. For example, the Industrial Revolution can be approached through science and technology, economic organisation, social impact, political consequences and so on. Few historians approach their subjects from a 'total' point of view. It is important to ask why the authors took this approach rather than that and what impact it had upon their conclusions.

(3) How has the author organised the book? What method of communication has the author used? Chronological narrative? Topical analysis? The contents page of the book is perhaps the best place to start when looking at this.

(4) What sources have been used and how well? A breadth of primary sources will give an author a clearer picture of a subject than a narrow concentration on a small number. A study of the English Civil War based

only on royalist sources is likely to be unbalanced in its interpretation. How recent are the secondary sources referred to in the bibliography? A book on Roman Britain published in 1981 was criticised by one reviewer for not referring to any secondary work after 1976.

(5) Who is the author? You need to place authors in their social and cultural environment. Have they published anything else? What was their training as – historian, sociologist, political scientist? This information is often found on the jackets of books.

(6) When was the book first published? A book published in 1984 on Attlee's 1945–51 government had greater access to cabinet papers than one published in 1960. Generally the more recent a book the more up-to-date its information. But you need to look out for books that have been reprinted without fundamental revision. For example Peter Mathias' excellent *The First Industrial Nation* was first published in 1969 and was reprinted many times before a second edition was published in 1983. He wrote that:

> Almost fourteen years have elapsed between the initial publication and this much-revised second edition. In the interim only such corrections as could be made without resetting pages were possible, so that the text has been more revised against than revised. Such has been the pace of new research that attrition has come swiftly even if (as one hopes) the book has grown old gracefully.

Examples: The Genesis of the Working Class

Look at the extracts below and analyse them in terms of subject, thesis and author.

(a) E. P. Thompson

This book has a clumsy title, but it is one which meets its purpose, *Making*, because it is a study of an active process, which owes much to agency as to conditioning. The working class did not rise like the sun at an appointed time. It was present at its own making.

    Class, rather than classes, for reasons which it is one purpose of this book to examine. There is, of course, a difference. 'Working classes' is a descriptive term, which evades as much as it defines. It ties loosely together a bundle of discrete phenomena. There were tailors here and weavers there, and together they make up the working classes. . . . The relationship must always be embodied in real people and in a real context.

    We cannot have love without lovers, nor deference without squires and labourers. And class happens when some men, as a result of common experiences (inherited or shared), feel and articulate the identity of their interests as between themselves, and as against other men whose interests are different from (and usually opposed to) theirs. . . . For I am convinced that we cannot understand class unless we see it as a social and cultural formation, arising from processes which can only be studied as they work themselves out over a considerable historical period. In the years between 1780 and 1832 most English working people came to feel an identity of interest as between themselves and as against their rulers and employers. . . . Thus the working–class presence was, in 1832, the most significant factor in British political life. . . . This is a group of studies, on related themes, rather than a consecutive narrative.

(E. P. Thompson, *The Making of the English Working Class*, Penguin edn, 1968, pp. 9, 10, 12)

(b) Harold Perkin

Some years ago I argued the case for social history as the vertebrate discipline built around a central organising theme, the history of society qua society, of social structure in all its manifold and constantly changing ramifications. I added that this kind of comprehensive social history should – indeed, could only – deal with one society at a time and over a finite period. By thus nailing my historical colours to the mast I took on the obligation of attempting such a comprehensive social history. This book is the result. . . . It concerns the emergence in England of that modern class society which we in the twentieth century have inherited from our Victorian predecessors, and are engaged in reshaping in ways which fall outside the compass of this volume. The origins of modern English society, as indeed of all modern developed and developing societies, go back to the seminal period both for Britain and the rest of the world which we inadequately call the Industrial Revolution. The central organising theme of the book is the belief that the Industrial Revolution was no mere sequence of changes in industrial techniques and production, but a social revolution with social causes and a social process as well as profound social effects. It was a revolution in human productivity, in the capacity of men to wring a living from nature, and therefore in both the number of human beings who could be supported on a given area of land and the abundance of their means and enjoyment of life. Since it was the first and only spontaneous industrial revolution of modern times, it required a society of a peculiar, not to say unique, kind to generate it, and the first three chapters lay out the problem of its causation, attempt to delineate the peculiarities and uniqueness, of pre-industrial society in England, and explain the specific ways in which, if it did not create, it at least drew together into productive harmony the traditional, economic, technological, intellectual and cultural causes of industrialism. . . . The most important social effects, however, and the heart of the book, are the growth of a new social structure within and its ultimate replacement of the old, the birth of a new society based on the horizontal solidarities of class in place of the old vertical connections of dependency and patronage (chapter VI), and its growth through the violent conflicts of its early nineteenth-century adolescence (chapters VII–IX). Finally chapter X explores the tensions between the ideal and the reality of this viable class society, and the underlying instability which brought it, by 1880, to the threatened loss of viability and a further round of social change.

(H. Perkin, *The Origins of Modern English Society 1780–1880*, London, 1969, pp. iv–v)

(c) John Foster

In many ways this study is experimental. Its subject is the labour movement in three nineteenth-century towns: Northampton, South Shields and (above all) Oldham. Its central theme is the development and decline of a revolutionary class consciousness in the second quarter of the century. But its basic aim goes beyond this: to further our understanding of how industrial capitalism developed *as a whole*. . . .

The study began with two sets of questions. The first concerned the problem of 'liberalization': the specific nature of the process which lay behind the new developments in the middle of the century. These first questions all involved the inside workings of a particular slice of English history (did it represent a process at all? Was it related to the preceding class consciousness? Why did it occur then and not later?) The other questions were more designed to place these developments in a larger perspective: to specify the changing content of mass consciousness against what came before and after: to reconstruct concrete forms as a basis for comparison elsewhere.

(J. Foster, *Class Struggle and the Industrial Revolution*, London, 1974, pp. 1, 251)

(d) Iowerth Prothero

This study focuses on working-class movements in London in the first four decades of the nineteenth century. . . . But London was not revolutionised, it was not a city of factories of thousand-man workshops, its industries remained small-scale in organisation and traditional in technology. A study of London workers' movements is therefore a study not of factory-workers or miners, but of workmen in the old, unmechanised handicraft trades – the artisans. This in no way diminishes its importance, quite the reverse. For few people then worked in factories. Even in 1850 England was not yet an industrialised country but one still undergoing industrialisation. . . . Factory workers were far outnumbered by skilled artisans. . . . Their continued numerical and social importance does not make the artisans at all a static object of study. On the contrary, they were experiencing great changes and were themselves changing. . . . The shipwrights of the Port of London were an especially important group of men, given the size of the great port and the fact that Britain was at war from 1793 to 1815. . . . The leader of the shipwrights, from about 1800 until his death in 1837, was John Gast. He is the central figure of the book, the focus of my study of London artisans. . . . A study of Gast becomes a way of studying the London artisans. . . . [But] it is axiomatic that we cannot understand such a figure without examining the situation of his trade. It is a particularly useful approach to take a member of a very aristocratic, unproletarianised trade, who was yet involved in these wider movements. It is also a very rewarding way of studying artisan activity, for my approach is emphatically not that of first classifying political outlooks in intellectual terms and subsequently seeking social explanations or labels for them. To understand the political involvement of artisans, we must first begin with their position, outlook, ideals and experience.

(I. Prothero, *Artisans and Politics in Early Nineteenth-Century London – John Gast and His Times*, London, 1979, pp. 1, 2, 4–6)

(e) Craig Calhoun

The most widespread, powerful, and radical social movements in the modern world have been of a type we may call 'populist'. They have been born and nurtured of attachments to tradition and community; they have seen an intimate connection between the immediate and local motivations of their actions and the less clear but larger and more lasting results at which they aimed. These movements have been consistently misunderstood by contemporary commentators, historians and social theorists. . . . The present work is something of a prologomenon to such rethinking of our theories of community, class and collective action, of revolution and popular protest. It is an attempt to explore systematically and in some detail the problem as it appears in one historical instance. The instance is that of Britain between Jacobinism and Chartism, from the 1790s to the 1840s. This is a critical instance for two reasons. First, it provided the empirical and experiential basis for the original development of the theory of working-class radicalism. Second, it has been a central focus of later empirical research shaped by the general theory. In order to elucidate the problems of using the theory in empirical analysis, I have focused a great deal of attention on a single work (E. P. Thompson's *The Making of the English Working Class*). . . . Although frequent reference is made to primary sources, the present work is not mainly concerned with adducing facts to settle purely empirical questions. It is, rather, concerned with what we are to make of facts which are, in large part, widely known and not in contest. This is an essay in and on historical interpretation, and few topics for interpretation are more hotly contested than the question of class struggle during the industrial revolution.

(C. Calhoun, *The Question of Class Struggle*, Basil Blackwell, 1982, pp. vii–viii, xiii)

How to Read Secondary Sources

Francis Bacon wrote that: 'Some books are to be tasted, others to be swallowed and some few to be chewed and digested.' So what are the best ways of approaching reading? To begin with your method of reading and your reading speed should vary according to your purpose. There are certain misconceptions about reading which need to be noted:

It is not essential to read every word.
Fast reading is not unnatural or bad for the eyes.
Very fast reading-speeds are possible.
Skim-reading is neither lazy nor dishonest.
Slow reading does not facilitate memory any more than fast reading. On any first reading only about 40 per cent of the material is digested regardless of the amount of time spent on it.

It is possible to identify five reading techniques which can be used.

   (i) 'Trial reading' – a quick survey so that you can decide whether the material is going to be of any real value to you. This is to some extent a subjective judgement and is something developed through experience.
  (ii) 'Scanning' – scan the contents and index to find the 'keywords' that you are concerned with. Find the correct pages and scan them looking for the words rather than actually reading them. This allows you to find the relevant sections or sentences.
 (iii) 'Skim-reading' – this lets you get a quick overview of the subject and identify the parts that are of immediate interest and, importantly, how they fit into the overall framework and thesis of the book.
  (iv) 'Rapid-reading – the purpose here can be both for pleasure and as part of active study (see Bibliography).

(v) 'Critical-reading' – the purpose is to allow you to weigh and consider, to evaluate and criticise the material. You might want to take notes at this time (see above, Chapter 1).

To summarise, your approach to reading needs to be active and to follow a logical pattern.

First, survey your material and consider your purpose.
Secondly, question yourself. Why should I read it? How should I read it?
Thirdly, read critically. Skim, reread, consider, select, make notes.
Fourthly, consider what you have done, review your work. Have you obtained all the information or ideas you want?
Finally, revise what you have done. Make your revision notes, listing the main points.

Further work

(1) Choose one of the books recommended to you and produce a synopsis of its main points. Compare this with those produced by your fellow students.
(2) How far does Francis Bacon's statement reflect your own practice?
(3) How can you 'gut' a book?
(4) How do you cope with different interpretations of the same subject?
(5) Secondary material for the historian means more than just history books and articles. Discuss.

7 *Debate and Controversy*

The past is at the same time both changeless and changing. Events that have occurred in the past cannot change. Magna Carta was signed, Julius Caesar was assassinated, the First World War did take place; but historical interpretation of those events and people does change. Historians develop new ways of looking at the past, alternative methods for examining evidence and undiscovered sources. These can all result in revisions of accepted orthodoxies. This chapter draws together the work on evidence and is concerned with three examples of debate and controversy in which the parameters and historical problems involved will be outlined.

Historians cannot be totally objective. They can only examine the available evidence as fairly as possible before coming to their conclusions: but the surviving records might be very limited, perhaps tempting the historian to attach too much importance to the detritus that has survived. This is clearly the case when considering Elizabeth I and her parliaments. On the other hand, the corpus of evidence may be so large and require such broad linguistic skills that no one historian can master it. The events leading to the First World War illustrate this logistical problem. Historians can fall foul of 'hindsight' and interpret events and situations knowing what happened afterwards. This was taken to extremes in the notion of the 'Whig interpretation of history' that pervaded much nineteenth- and some twentieth-century historical writing. Herbert Butterfield wrote in his critique of this view of the past first published in 1931 that: 'It is part and parcel of the whig interpretation of history that it studies the past with reference to the present. . . . The whig historian stands on the summit of the twentieth century and organises his scheme of history from the point of view of his own day.' and that 'we study the past for the sake of the present.' Historians too are influenced, like everyone else, by the world in which they live, the events surrounding them and their own beliefs and prejudices. A Marxist historian perceives the world in a different way from a liberal or conservative one, a Soviet historian from an American one. The inaccessibility of the past necessitates diversity of perspective and interpretation.

(1) Examine your own view of the past in relation to the points made above.

(2) Too much historical evidence is as bad as too little. Discuss.

(3) History is both changing and changeless. Account for this paradox.

(4) Why can there never be a 'true' account of past events and actions?

(5) The Whig interpretation of history was an attractive way of looking at the past. Why do you think this was so?

Debate 1. The Parliaments of Elizabeth I

Until about 1920 it was generally agreed that Parliament played a very small, 'subservient' role in sixteenth-century government which centred on strong, autocratic monarchy. This view was challenged by A. F. Pollard and especially by Sir John Neale. Pollard viewed the history of Parliament as a long-term evolutionary process towards the ideals of Common's supremacy and democracy. Wallace Notstein had added little in his *The Winning of the Initiative by the House of Commons* published in 1924. He concentrated on the development of procedures in the Commons which, he argued, had a sinister political motive, maintaining that they were intended to weaken the control of the Privy Councillors on the Commons and to give greater freedom to the opponents of royal policies. Neale also believed in a markedly evolutionary scheme for the history of Tudor Parliament from the underdevelopment of the Middle Ages to 'maturity' under Elizabeth in terms of privilege, procedure and political role. Neale openly declared that he intended to seek out the origins of the Stuart conflict in the sixteenth century. In *The Elizabethan House of Commons* (1949) and his two-volume *Elizabeth I and her Parliaments* (1953, 1957) Neale drew a dramatic picture. Parliament's power increased. There was a shift of authority from Lords to Commons. The Lords lost its age-old superiority and independence and became a dutiful, obedient servant of the Crown. Its prime function became one of assisting the Crown 'in controlling the Commons'. In contrast, the Commons became increasingly willing to assert itself, to question royal policy and to oppose the government. It even became willing, Neale argued, to impose its own policies on the Crown. This opposition was portrayed as the 'apprenticeship' of the early Stuart sessions. Geoffrey Elton has recently argued that Neale believed that 'the reign of Elizabeth witnessed the rise of the Commons just in time to get ready for the battle with the Stuart kings. Indeed he thought he saw Elizabethan rehearsals for that political conflict.' The growth of conflict, orchestrated by a persistent Puritan opposition organised to implement its own programme, was the central theme of his two-volume work. Elton again:

> Neale's Parliament – or, rather, his House of Commons – fitted neatly into the received story of a growth from the supposedly acquiescent assemblies of Henry VIII's reign to the supposedly recalcitrant assemblies of the early seventeenth century.

This view of Elizabeth's Parliaments has recently come under close scrutiny and Neale's orthoxies have been revised. It is important to note that Neale did get some things right. His narrative of parliamentary events is often correct in detail if suspect in interpretation. His work on the expansion of constituencies and election disputes is still accepted. The Commons did acquire a degree of social homogeneity. But in important respects Neale's interpretations were misplaced and fitted into the whiggish mode. Parliament was a trinity, not a duet of Queen and Commons. The evidence makes it clear that the Lords were not only an active part of the Parliament, deeply engaged in the work of legislation, but also willing to oppose the Queen's wishes. In 1559 members of the Lords, especially the bishops, opposed the religious settlement. It was more productive than the Commons: a higher proportion of bills that originated there became law. For example, in the 1563 Parliament it initiated 43 out of the 135 bills of which 32 became Acts compared to only 19 of the 90 bills which became Acts from the Commons. There is little doubt that the Lords was an efficient chamber, small and able to examine bills very closely. The Lords should not be either ignored or underestimated during Elizabeth's reign.

The main plank of Neale's thesis lay in his identification of opposition which, he maintained, was as much a parliamentary dynamic in Elizabeth's reign as it was to become in 1640–2. He pointed to the willingness of the Commons to challenge the royal prerogative over monopolies in 1597 and 1601 and the emergence of Puritan opposition to religious policies. Certainly there was irritation from a war-weary Parliament when Elizabeth's economies extended to monopolies which cost her nothing but which cost the nation dear. In 1597 Parliament grumbled but Elizabeth took little notice. The reassembly of Parliament in 1601 saw the earlier rumblings transformed into an open attack on monopolies and a lengthy debate in which the Crown's power to grant them was questioned. This pressure led to Elizabeth promising that harmful monopolies would be examined by the courts. But this episode was an expression of widespread discontent in the constituencies which MPs represented. The monopolies issue can be seen as opposition by local government to the demands of war imposed by central government.

The whole notion of a Puritan opposition group which Neale put forward depended on two unfounded assumptions: that in 1559 the more extreme Protestants exercised a decisive influence on the religious settlement and that a list of some 43 MPs in 1566 who were active in that year's succession agitation was seen by Neale as the hard-core Puritan opposition. This led to Neale using a circular argument. Leading MPs were identified as Puritans and consequently what they did became Puritan activities.

Neale's argument on the Parliament of 1559 was that it developed into a struggle between a Conservative Queen and a radical Puritan pressure group. It is generally agreed that the outcome of the contest was a compromise in which the Queen conceded rather more than her opponents. But to Neale there was an opposition which he could not test because no known list of members survived. These conclusions have recently been drastically modified by Norman Jones in his *Faith by Statute: Parliament and the Settlement of Religion, 1559* (London, 1982). He found that Puritanism was not a potent force. What resistance there was to the government's programme came from the Catholic bishops and some of the Catholic peers in the House of Lords. Jones found that Elizabeth obtained more or less what she wanted from the religious settlement. She was a realist and gained about as much as she could reasonably have expected. Neale came to similar conclusions about the Parliaments of 1563–7 and 1571. He argued that opposition had a positive programme, developed tactics and a planned campaign of action. There was only one flaw with this interpretation: it did not fit the evidence. He claimed to have discovered an organised party which campaigned for Elizabeth to marry or settle the succession in 1563–7 and which advocated church reform in 1566–7 and 1571. His conclusion was based upon his reading of the list of forty-three members in the form of a doggerel which referred to them as 'our choir'. Historians have come to accept some of them as Puritans – Paul Wentworth, Robert Bell, William Strickland – but on Neale's say so. Recent analysis of the list tells a different story. The list covers a broad spectrum of people, few of whom were radical Protestants. Neale did not explain what he meant by a 'Puritan'. If a 'Puritan' meant someone who hated Popes, feared Catholicism and wanted to improve the standards of the new Anglican church then most of those named in the list were Puritans. But, with the exceptions of Wentworth and Strickland, the views of Neale's 'Puritan choir' were indistinguishable from the Privy Council and Archbishop Matthew Parker. So if the list was not one of Puritans what was it? There are powerful internal arguments that it was a piece of doodling written about MPs that caught an anonymous member's eye. 'Choir' can then mean, not a harmonious organisation, but the fact that these men were vocal, noisy, the natural leaders –

> Bell the Orator
> Wentworth the Wrangler
> Saint John the Jangler
> Brown the Blasphemer
> . . .
> As for the rest
> they be at devotion
> and when they be prest
> they crye a good motion.

– whom the Commons looked to for a lead in debate. Nowhere is there a single hint that this document has any connection with Puritanism. On the basis of this document Neale erected the Puritan choir and supported it with a framework of inference and assumption. But assumption, even with Neale's statement that 'it would take a simpleton not to suspect a planned drive' by the choir, does not constitute valid historical interpretation.

Historians accept that there is much in Neale that is now questionable. Certainly the disquiet over the state of the Church and the threat to Protestantism was not the property of Puritans determined to form an opposition in the Commons. Councillors, bishops, people in government all expressed the same concerns. Christopher Haigh, in the conclusion of a collection of essays he edited, '*The Reign of Elizabeth I*' (1985), wrote that

> It is the fate of those who have dominated a subject to be attacked by those who come after – as it is the fate of those who stand on a giant's shoulder to be accused of trampling him down. . . . The academic 'controversy', is the historian's natural milieu, his equivalent of the scientist's laboratory and symposium. Only by debate can history be kept alive.

The question of Elizabethan Parliaments illustrates the following problems facing historians

(1) The dominance of one historian whose conclusions were based on a detailed discussion of the sources and who establishes the orthodox position. Citing Neale gave authority to any discussion before the 1970s.

(2) A re-examination of this orthodoxy, questioning the validity of interpretation which leads eventually to the creation of a new orthodoxy.

Why was Neale able to maintain his position for so long? What was the basis of his dominance? How has his interpretation been modified? Events are multi-dimensional and examining them from a different perspective can lead to attractive, tenable conclusions being reached.

Debate 2. The Causes of the First World War

> Yes, we needed it. We *needed* the war! Not for the Serbs' sake, but for our own salvation! Because we have lost confidence in ourselves, we've become decrepit, we've sunk so low that we can't go any lower. . . . We need some great *exploit*, so that we can renew ourselves! We need victory, to freshen the atmosphere – we're stifling!
>
> (A. Solzhenitsyn, *August 1914*, pp. 563–4)

There are several ways of isolating the causes of wars: some historians have used 'long-term', 'short-term' and 'immediate' to codify events in time, while Lawrence Stone used the more sociological terms of 'preconditions', 'precipitants' and 'triggers'. How far back should the historian seek antecedents of a conflict? Are the origins of the First and Second World Wars to be sought not only in European, and specifically German, history of the twentieth century, but also in the militarism of the mediaeval Teutonic knights or Frederick the Great? At what point does conflict become 'inevitable'? With the railway timetables of a military plan?

Causation is a complex field, where issues and personalities must be weighed and assessed. There is considerable room for discussion and debate, because historians are also influenced by the opinion of their time: the most gloomy conclusions on the impact of the Thirty Years' War on Germany were written in the 1930s when Europe was suffering from economic depression and the aftermath of the First World War.

As well as new ways of looking at evidence there is also 'new' evidence, particularly in the twentieth century where controversial, sensitive or damaging material may be kept secret until released under a 'thirty-year rule' or by a less scrupulous form of government, or after a statesman's death. Yet much remains uncertain or shrouded in obscurity, particularly where historians seek to enter the minds of distant generations; this may engender a feeling that debate is purely subjective, based solely on value judgements. As one historian ironically wrote on the Partition of Africa: 'Well, it just happened that way – the coincidental result of several independent chains of events, each with multiple causes.'

Ronald Hyam wrote that 'there is no such thing as finality in historical explanation, and thus there is no theory or interpretation which may not one day be revised or even disproved totally. New evidence does not necessarily have to come to light for this to happen. The process is almost invariably started by some quite modest thought, by exercising a bit of common sense and adopting a fresh angle of vision.'

The first European debate is on the Origins of the First World War. To enter this debate – as any other – a firm background knowledge of the events is required, as in L. C. F. Turner, *Origins of the First World War* (1984). Do not turn to a compilation of specialised articles such as H. W. Koch (ed.), *The Origins of the First World War* (1984), until you have begun to discover what the main themes of the debate are.

During the interwar period the 'war guilt question' or, in the German polemical view, the 'war guilt lie' (*Kriegsschuldlüge*) was highly controversial. The debate was stimulated by Article 231 of the Treaty of Versailles:

> The Allied and Associated Governments affirm and Germany accepts the responsibility of Germany and her allies for causing all the loss and damage to which the Allies and Associated Governments and their nationals have been subjected as a consequence of the war imposed upon them by the aggression of Germany and her allies.

German historians and the 'War Guilt Section' of the German Foreign Ministry set out to prove that Germany was not solely responsible for causing the war, although that was not what Article 231 said! Each government also began to publish *selected* documents on the war – perhaps prompted by the Russian Bolsheviks' publication of the secret treaties between the Allies – and a consensus gradually emerged that the war had been due less to evil intent than to stupidity. 'The nations slithered over the brink into the boiling cauldron of war without any trace of apprehension or dismay', as Lloyd George put it. This conveniently let the Germans off the hook by implying mutual responsibility of victor and vanquished on a wide range of issues: Balkan nationalism; the network of great power alliances; the colonial scramble; the naval race; the French desire for *revanche* after 1871; the mobilisation plans (including the famous Schlieffen plan); the role of the military or 'a deep-seated malaise of international society – "the European anarchy" or "the contradictions of capitalism"' (H. R. Trevor-Roper). It was a chain reaction with short-term causes in Africa and the Balkans triggered off by the assassination of Archduke Franz Ferdinand in June 1914. Misunderstandings and decades of suspicion and hostility prevented diplomatic resolution of the crisis, as Sir Edward Grey strove for.

The advent of Nazism and the Second World War seemed to confirm that a hasty condemnation of Germany's part in the causes of the First World War had merely exacerbated the position: it had helped to produce Hitler. He was, of course, the guilty man in the origins of the Second World War. As Hugh Trevor-Roper said: 'The Second World War was Hitler's personal war in many senses. He intended it, he prepared for it, he chose the moment for launching it.'

It was, perhaps, all too convenient. In 1961 the German historian Fritz Fischer published *Griff nach der Weltmacht* (translated as *Germany's Aims in the First World War*, 1967). Fischer's highly controversial thesis was that there was no conflict of view between the military and political rulers of Germany in 1914 – both wanted war at a favourable opportunity to break open the encirclement by Germany's enemies and so become a 'world power' (*Weltmacht*). The background to this was *Weltpolitik*, and in the 1914 crisis Fischer claimed that Germany was setting the pace, not Austria–Hungary.

Fischer based his ideas on the war plans of Germany *during* the war; these were expansionist, as in the case of Chancellor Bethmann-Hollweg's September 1914 Programme, but were designed for when Germany won the war. Were they though the *cause* of the conflict? Fischer's argument was that these heady imperialist ideas were evident in governmental as well as military circles in Germany before 1914: Germany was to resort to war to establish herself as a world power alongside the other world powers which had achieved their position before Germany had achieved national unity. The world, or at least part of it, would therefore be organised in such a way that it should be dominated by Germany, and serve her economic, cultural and strategic interests. The German government, even if they did not actually want war in 1914, were prepared to face the *risk* of it to pursue their general aims, and encouraged Austria–Hungary to provoke war then, even if it could not be localised. Certainly the peace treaty signed with Bolshevik Russia at

Brest–Litovsk in March 1918 was expansionist, favouring Fischer's thesis of annexation.

Much of the historical debate on Fischer's book (the *polemical* debate raged fiercely in the media!) centred on documents and personalities. (Fischer tried to go beyond the diplomatic sources which tended to conceal aggression anyway.) At least part of the interpretation of the documents depended on the interpretation of character. Was Bethmann-Hollweg's statement in 1912 that 'from many indications [it is] at least doubtful whether England would actively intervene if Russia and France appear directly as provoking the war', to be taken at face value or, as the historian Gerhard Ritter wrote, was it a tactical point to calm the Kaiser and resist German naval increases?

This is where the historian demonstrates his skill and experience by *understanding* as well as reading, and it is here that the historical process reaches its zenith. Of course, some documentary evidence can never be unravelled; as James Joll wrote, what tone of voice did the Russian Foreign Minister Sazonov use in 1914 when he heard the news of the Austrian ultimatum to Serbia and said, '*C'est la guerre européenne*'? Regret, relief or surprise?

A. J. P. Taylor placed great reliance on the mobilisation of troop trains as the key to 'the war by timetable' as he explained it in a typically clever little article. He was rightly chided by Imanuel Geiss: 'The famous mechanism of mobilisation and railway time-tables is often taken as an excuse for not troubling to find out what really happened in July 1914 before this mechanism had set in.' Geiss, a disciple of Fischer, stressed German pressure on her ally as the key to the events of 1914.

If these were the 'triggers' what about the 'preconditions' and 'precipitants'? Fischer's answer to his critics was *Krieg der Illusionen* (1969), translated as *War of Illusions: German Policies from 1911 to 1914* (1975), which presented the importance of domestic politics overriding foreign affairs – *der Primat der Innenpolitik*. In this view an overwhelming desire to preserve the social and political order from democracy, Socialism and other elements required a strong military hold on affairs. Fischer was a bold man because there was a deep feeling that he had somehow betrayed the interests of his countrymen by revealing uncomfortable facts about Germany's imperial past; indeed the Adenauer government tried to silence Fischer, condemned his work and even attempted to prevent him from lecturing on it in America. The attempt failed. Fischer's retort was that historical truth was of greater importance than *raison d'état*. One of his other works, translated in 1975, was *Weltmacht oder Niedergang, World Power or Decline: The Controversy over Germany's Aims in the First World War*, in which Fischer stated his views in seven theses:

(1) German wartime aims were the logical extension of pre-war aspirations for world power.

(2) The German government consciously provoked – rather than just risked – war in July 1914 for domestic and diplomatic reasons.

(3) The September 1914 war aims programme remained the blueprint throughout the war.

(4) and (5). German policy in wartime is best understood as a consistent and active commitment to expansion.

(6) These aspirations were shared by the mass of Germans.

(7) Military victory was seen by most members of the German ruling class as a means for preserving the conservative political system.

Volker Berghahn in *Germany and the Approach of War in 1914* (1973) stressed *Innenpolitik*, in particular the use of a large navy to offset the disappointing absence of large colonies – 'Tirpitz's naval policy was nothing less than an ambitious plan to stabilise the Prusso-German political system and to paralyse the pressure for change' – the problems of armaments and finance, the theme of risks – World Power or Decline – and a situation by 1912 which 'brought the Reich perilously close to complete internal paralysis and diplomatic stagnation'. He noted the gloom of 1912–14, the small number of people involved in decision-making in 1914, and the 'cunning manoeuvre of political deception' by the governing élite in 1914.

So where does this lead? According to Jacques Droz, Hitler could not have come to power so easily if German historians had not deceived the public, both during and after the First World War, about Germany's aims in that war, and if they had not lent support to the power politics and expansionist aspirations of Wilhelminian imperialism. Historians seem to bear a heavy burden whether they conceal or reveal.

Examples of the evidence may be helpful. In December 1912 at a top-level meeting in Berlin, Tirpitz (according to Admiral von Müller) 'made the observation that the navy would prefer to see the postponement of the great fight for one-and-a-half years. Moltke [Army C. in C.] says the navy would not be ready even then and the army would get into an increasingly unfavourable position, for the enemies were arming more strongly than we.'

In what different ways might this be interpreted?

In May or June 1914 – he was not sure which – Gottlieb von Jagow, German Foreign Secretary, discussed the military situation with Moltke:

Moltke described to me his opinion of our military situation. The prospects of the future oppressed him heavily. In two to three years Russia would have completed her armaments. The military superiority of our enemies would then be so great that he did not know how he could overcome them. Today we would still be a match for them. In his opinion there was no alternative to making preventive war in order to defeat the enemy while we still had a chance of victory.

Prince Philipp zu Eulenburg-Hertenfeld (German ambassador in Vienna, 1894–1902) wrote to Professor Kurt Breysig in September 1919 about events in July 1914:

Serbia *is* Russia. If Austria marches against Serbia, and *if Berlin does not prevent Austria's belligerent action*, then the great breaking wave of World War rolls irresistibly towards us. I repeat: Berlin *must* know that, otherwise *idiots* live in the Wilhelmstrasse. Kaiser Wilhelm *must* know that.

If Austria takes the step upon which she has decided at the Cabinet meeting of 7 July, and if Kaiser Wilhelm assures Austria of his loyalty to the Alliance *under any circumstances*, then he also *shares* Count Berchtold's policy with regard to war *with Russia* – and Russia is the ally of France.

The situation that I have briefly described here is an established fact that cannot be masked.

(quoted in J. C. G. Röhl [ed.] *1914: Delusion or Design*, 1973, pp. 134–5)

So did the politicians in Berlin see 1914 as a means of launching not merely a local but a general war? Was this for preventive or aggressive purposes? For internal or external motives? As Karl-Heinz Janssen wrote in 1972: 'What Fritz Fischer . . . had only been able to surmise on the basis of a few sparse notes and letters has now become a certainty:

Germany not only unleashed the Second World War; her leaders also began the First World War, if not through deliberate planning, then at least through running a conscious risk – in full awareness of the dangers.

Further points worth considering are the importance of Social Darwinism, the role of various groups in the government – the Court, the Army, the Navy, the Chancellor and the Foreign Office – the deliberate manipulation, suppression and even destruction of evidence by the Weimar Republic in the 1920s *and* by later governments. In the mid-1960s 'the pre-1914 diaries of the Head of the Kaiser's Navy Cabinet were published in a carefully expurgated version' (J. C. G. Röhl). Perhaps this is not surprising: the theme of continuity in German history from Bismarck to Hitler must have been very unsettling for many Germans, destroying, as Fischer wrote, 'many a treasured illusion'. Yet it is the historian's task to be sceptical and questioning. How much are statesmen 'affected by current ideas and preconceptions, by the social and administrative structure, by the political and economic "realities" of the situation?' (L. L. Farrar). How is foreign policy conceived? How are ends affected by means? How do circumstances alter aims? How do wars begin? What is the relationship between policy and public opinion? Was there any alternative for Germany – a giant among its neighbours – other than aggressive policies? What were the plans and policies of the other major European powers?

What have *you* learned from this debate, and how does it relate to debates within the period of history that you are studying?

Debate 3. Social and Economic Effects of the Thirty Years War

The war solved no problem. Its effects, both immediate and indirect, were either negative or disastrous. Morally subversive, economically destructive, socially degrading, confused in its causes, devious in its course, futile in its result, it is the outstanding example in European history of meaningless conflict.

(C. V. Wedgwood, *The Thirty Years War*, 1938 [1964 edn, p. 526])

Written history usually reflects something of the time in which it was composed. I wrote this book in the later nineteen thirties when the depression, the Hitler regime in Germany and the Spanish War made the plight of the hungry, the displaced, the persecuted and the exiled an ever-present concern. . . . The suffering caused by the Thirty Years War was beyond all reckoning. . . . But it must also be remembered that the Thirty Years War and its supposed consequences have become a popular myth in German history. Every calamity – economic, moral and social – is apt to be ascribed to the effects of this conflict. Such exaggerated views are misleading. The long-term effects of the war differed in different parts of the country and all generalizations are suspect.'

(Ibid, [Foreword, p. 7])

This debate is not on the causes of war but on its social and economic aftermath. The Thirty Years War was protracted (1618, but more correctly 1619, to 1648) yet very few powers were involved for the entire period, and not all areas of Western and Central Europe were equally affected by the fighting. As Wedgwood pointed out, there are dangers in exaggeration and generalisation, and contemporary propaganda was guilty of both. Here is Grimmelshausen in *Simplicius Simplicissimus* (1668):

The first thing that the riders did was to stable their horses. After that each one started his own business which indicated nothing but ruin and destruction. While some started to slaughter, cook and fry . . . others stormed through the house from top to bottom as if the golden fleece of Colchis were hidden there. Others again took linen, clothing and other goods . . .; what they did not want was broken up and destroyed. . . . Others smashed the ovens and windows as if to announce an eternal summer. . . . Our maid had been treated in the stable in such a way that she could not leave it any more – a shameful thing to tell. They bound the farm-hand and laid him on the earth, put a clamp of wood in his mouth and emptied a milking churn full of horrid dung water into his belly. This they called the Swedish drink.

(quoted in G. M. Best, *Seventeenth Century Europe*, 1982, p. 23)

But was it such an unmitigated disaster? In 1966 S. H. Steinberg suggested that the two world wars of the twentieth century had revealed the evidence of the Thirty Years War in a new light (*The Thirty Years War*). He stressed four main themes:

(1) Atrocity accusations from the First World War usually revealed the extent of propaganda, so perhaps cannibalism stories during the Thirty Years War should be discounted.
(2) The German hyperinflation of 1919–23 has clarified the significance of the German inflation of 1619–22.
(3) The recovery of cities like Coventry, Hamburg and Dresden showed how devastating war could be and yet how these places could so soon be transformed and reconstructed.

(4) Historians blamed the war for problems which may have been present before it started, or were exacerbated by the failure of politicians *after* the war. (This is also referred to as the fallacy of *post hoc ergo propter hoc* – to say that something happened *after* an event is not to say that it was caused by it.)

Steinberg also claimed that much of the evidence came from those who suffered most, generally the educated professional men who had most to lose, for example 'ministers of religion whose persons and property were always the easiest targets'. He emphasised the absence of statistical data on population, production and finances – war damage claims could be grossly inflated. So Steinberg offered a 'revisionist' interpretation, assembling 'a mosaic of details' rather than an overall picture.

He 'reduced' the mortality rate to an average of 6–8 per cent and criticised poor, even naïve, interpretations of population statistics; epidemics, he said, were greater killers than warfare, although armies spread disease in their wake. Country areas may have suffered *temporary* falls in population because displaced persons moved into the comparative safety of walled towns. (*Mutatis mutandis*, London experienced a decrease of two million people between 1938 and 1946, but this does not mean that two million Londoners died during the war.) Steinberg even asserted that some places profited by the wars, especially armament centres like Essen.

Steinberg also noted fundamental changes in the German economy *before* the wars began, especially the long-term decline in south German towns like Augsburg which were oriented to the Mediterranean trade, and the commensurate growth of Baltic and North Sea ports and their hinterland – especially Hamburg.

East of the river Elbe Steinberg blamed the *Junkers* for the eviction of peasant proprietors, although the demand for cereals and cattle for the armies may have accelerated this process.

In conclusion, Leipzig was offered as an example of how a city could recover: it was besieged five times, captured by both sides, and suffered two major battles outside its gates, yet Leipzig overtook all other south German cities and became a leading trade centre with its twice-yearly fairs.

Steinberg's general conclusion was that setbacks in one area were offset by gains elsewhere, and that if Germany seemed to be suffering it was only in relation to other European countries developing faster. He denied colossal losses of population, complete economic ruin and the collapse of civilisation – they were myths.

Was this too optimistic, too revisionist, even oversimplified? There were some who thought that Steinberg had gone too far: for example, was not recovery after the Second World War heavily assisted by governmental aid – the Marshall Plan – rather than self-help? And there *were* serious atrocities during the First World War: at Andenne in Belgium in 1914 the town was burned down and 110 inhabitants shot; in Lorraine, at Noméry, the town was soaked in petrol and set ablaze to force the population into the open; and during the cold March of 1918 50,000 inhabitants of Saint-Quentin were sent into eastern Belgium, into the Ardennes, and elsewhere. On one occasion eleven Englishmen hiding in a house were shot together with the head of the household who had hidden them, and a neighbour who had helped was sent to prison. These, and many others, are verifiable and not mere propaganda. (See 'France Occupied', *History Today*, October 1983, pp. 50–2.)

Subsequent participants in the debate stressed the complexity and variations of the geographical area known as Germany. Regional differences might prove to be more fruitful than all-embracing explanations. Henry Kamen adopted this line of thought and extended it to ask whether in economic aspects Germany was unique in this period or typical of Europe in general.

In his article ('The Economic and Social Consequences of the Thirty Years' War', *Past & Present*, 39, 1968) Kamen asked whether 'it is not possible to speak of the decline of Germany, but only of the decline of certain selected areas of Germany, some of which may have suffered from long-term factors of decay, while others were directly and physically annihilated by the war.' Secondly, like Steinberg, he claimed it to be unrealistic to differentiate between pre-war and wartime decline. Thirdly, he stated that the pre-war crisis centring on 1620 was of European, even worldwide, proportions.

It is often of value when examining a debate to study points of agreement as well as controversy among contributors. Kamen agreed with Steinberg that the war accentuated the decline of south German towns like Augsburg, allowing commercial hegemony to pass to the trade outlets of the north-west. However Kamen claimed that 'there can be no doubt at all that the war was a disaster for most of the German-speaking lands. The material devastation caused in Germany was enormous.' He agreed with Steinberg on population *displacement* rather than loss through death, and cited Günther Franz that over the German lands as a whole the urban centres lost one-third of their population and the rural areas lost 40 per cent. The problem is to assess how much of this was attributable to the war. (In the county of Lippe, only moderately hit by the war, the population fell by 35 per cent from 40,220 to 26,000 between 1618 and 1648.) Like Steinberg, Kamen agreed on the virility of plague, especially 1634–9: in 1635 Frankfurt had 6,943 deaths through plague. Plague was endemic in seventeenth-century Europe, but armies brought pestilence in their wake. In addition, the birth-rate fell, creating a manpower problem after the war.

Kamen also agreed with Steinberg on the uneven spread of disaster; among the areas that benefited were Lübeck, Hamburg, Bremen, Lower Saxony and towns in the Ruhr. He too used Essen and Leipzig as examples of prosperity or recovery. But he differed in his emphasis on the countryside suffering more than the towns. His point was that 'wartime disruption forced many independent peasants to leave the countryside for the cities' and dependent peasants willingly left the land to avoid labour obligations. Thus there was a labour shortage forcing wages up: labour became far more profitable than land, encouraging peasants to become day-labourers. Nobles and landlords could thus buy land cheaply, and even peasant communities could not resist because of exorbitant interest rates. 'Both individually and communally', Kamen wrote, 'the peasantry were ushered into a period of economic ruin.' This was especially true in Mecklenburg and Pomerania – in one district of the former nearly three-quarters of peasant holdings fell into noble hands.

Some rulers, as in Saxony, bought land to prevent the nobility doing this. Kamen stressed that the nature of rule was very important, whether in Germany, France, or elsewhere. A strong ruler could improve the status of the peasantry, as in Lower Saxony or Brandenburg. But where this was not the case the state of the peasantry worsened. As Kamen wrote, 'The feudal reaction provoked by the Thirty Years' War was not confined to German lands alone: it occurred wherever the war struck, in French territory or, at one remove, in imperialist Sweden.'

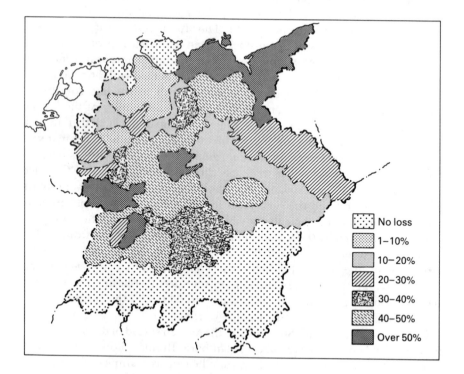

Figure 7.1

What conclusions may be tentatively drawn? By looking at studies of hundreds of localities Kamen believed that 'there is still no reason to discount the reality of devastation, plague, famine and sheer barbarism of the soldiery.' His example of population loss (Figure 7.1) does not speak for itself (few documents do), but it indicates the scale of the problem. (H. Kamen, *The Iron Century: Social Change in Europe 1550–1660*, 1971.) As Harold (now Lord) Wilson once said of unemployment, the national level may be so many per cent but for the unemployed it is 100 per cent. Law and Order were also at risk during internecine conflict, allowing peasant revolts in certain areas against the short- and long-term causes of their misery. There were vast numbers of refugees: Bohemia had a population of only 930,000 in 1648 compared with 1,700,000 before the war. Kamen tried here to differentiate between what was caused by the war and what developed from circumstances arising out of the war – a difficult distinction.

So as the debate stands neither the 'traditional' nor 'revisionist' viewpoint holds the field. Both new evidence and new understanding of evidence have revealed the complexity of the problem, and the example of the two world wars has enabled historians to stretch their imaginations into a European Civil War in the seventeenth century.

As with the nineteenth-century 'Standard of Living' controversy there are 'optimists' and 'pessimists'. The historian will encounter them in many aspects of economic history and must take as much from either as he can. There will be similar problems too with statistics, the geographical scope, selection of material and areas of agreement: but then history, as the Dutch historian Pieter Geyl said, 'is an argument without end'.

8 History – Nature and Variety

Everything is the sum of its past and nothing is comprehensible except through its history.

(Pierre Teilhard de Chardin)

The Meaning of History

History is generally something that historians 'do' rather than theorise about. It is a practical activity. This chapter is concerned with the nature of history and the variety of expertise which historians can draw upon. There is no real need for consensus about what should actually be examined or why. The quotations below indicate the diversity of views that historians have expressed. There may be some agreement about the parameters of history – past events – and the subject – people in society – and that the concern of historians should be with reconstructing the past. But that is about as far as it goes. What justification is there for studying the past? What is the relationship between history and other subjects? Is there a philosophy of history?

In every respect women's participation in history has been marginalized. Feminist history releases women from their obscurity as the wives, mothers and daughters of working men.

(Sally Alexander)

The history of all hitherto existing societies is the history of class struggles.

(Karl Marx)

The subject matter of history is human affairs, men in action, things which have happened and how they happened; concrete events fixed in time and space, and their grounding in the thoughts and feelings of men – not things universal and generalized; events as complex and diversified as the men who wrought them, those rational beings whose knowledge is seldom sufficient, whose ideas are but distantly related to reality, and who are never moved by reason alone.

(Sir Lewis Namier)

The subject matter of history is not the past as such, but the past for which we have evidence.

(R. G. Collingwood)

History is the continuous interaction between the historian and his facts, an unending dialogue between the present and the past.

(E. H. Carr)

The scope of history has gradually widened till it has come to include every aspect of the life of humanity . . . [the historian] must see life steadily and see it whole.

(G. P. Gooch)

History, as the study of the past, makes the coherence of what happened comprehensible by reducing events to a dramatic pattern and seeing them in a simple form.

(Johann Huizinga)

(1) Why are there so many different meanings of history?
(2) Is history just a story?
(3) How can we see the past as a whole?
(4) How far is history 'an unending dialogue between the present and the past'?

The past is chaos. History is literally a load of rubbish. That is what much evidence is. Historians impose an order, logic and reason upon people and events in the past which were anything but rational. History is a process but as Marc Bloch wrote, 'history is neither watchmaking nor cabinet construction. It is an endeavour towards better understanding.' Understanding comes through recreating past events. History is a 'synoptic' discipline in that it should allow everyone to take a general view of the whole past. Understanding of the present and the potential of the future is impossible without a sense of time. In all spheres of life, from personal relationships to political judgement, people constantly interpret their experience in this temporal perspective, whether they are conscious of it or not. George Kitson Clark has said that a person 'who ignores history will make the historical assumptions which are implicit in most language and in all political judgements but, he will not know he is making them and so will be unable to criticise them or reconsider the evidence on which they are based.'

History is collective memory, the storehouse of experience through which individuals develop a sense of their own social identity and their future prospects. It is to society what remembered experience is to the individual. History alerts people to the sheer variety and breadth of human achievements and thoughts. This may provide some realisation of the range of possibilities open to people. The value of history goes beyond this by developing imagination. History is a source of precedent and prediction. Comparisons across time do illuminate the present by highlighting what is recurrent and what is new, what is durable, transient and contingent in the present condition. Drawing historical analogies is a habitual and unavoidable part of the human condition. Above all history provides a critique of the myths that pervade and pervert society. Through historical analysis people can counteract propaganda which is often a selection from the past to justify present actions. History can liberate the individual from the problems of the present by providing an alternative scenario of the possible futures. It is little wonder that in many countries history and historians are or have been viewed with suspicion and are controlled. Nikita Khrushchev wrote that: 'Historians are dangerous people. They are capable of upsetting everything. They must be directed.'

(1) Are historians 'dangerous people'? What arguments can you put forward for historians being 'directed'?
(2) In what ways is the role of history different in communist and western democratic societies? Account for these differences.
(3) Why do historians 'pervert' the past and for what reasons?
(4) History is often called upon to justify present and future actions. How legitimate is this?

History – Science or Art?

At the beginning of this century there was a debate between those historians who saw their subject as a science and those who saw it as an art. J. B. Bury maintained that 'History is a science no less and no more' as did his French counterpart Fustel de Coulanges: 'History is and should be a science'. But just how valid was and is this distinction? Science, it is argued, is concerned with establishing general truths. Scientific method is objective, rational and detached using observation and controlled experiment. It is empirical. The scientist measures and tests and when a known cause continues to produce the same effect then it is justifiable to 'deduce' a scientific law. Through repeated experiment the scientist can confirm the 'truth' of a particular thing. E. H. Carr provided a useful list of reasons for distinguishing between art and science in 1964:

(a) history deals with the unique and science with the general;
(b) history is unable to predict;
(c) history teaches no lessons;
(d) history is of necessity subjective since people are observing themselves;
(e) history, unlike science, involves issues of religion and morality.

History is always of a tentative nature. There are inherent limitations in both evidence and historians' interpretations based on that evidence. Past events are unique and unrepeatable. They have taken place and had a concrete existence in time. Historians cannot run the event again to achieve the precision which a physicist can when ascertaining the laws of motion. Historians cannot establish general laws for the past even though some attempt to do so. Historians are concerned with specific episodes in the past that are concrete and unique. Paul Valéry said that: 'History is the science of what never happens twice'. Historical truth is therefore not absolute but interpretative. Historians can never detach themselves totally from the events they describe. Historical objectivity lies in the judicious critique of evidence, not in any empirical generalisation. We can examine the scientist's statistics and run the tests again. We have to rely on the historian's integrity. However, just to dismiss the question and accept Carr's solution is perhaps misleading. History does share more with science than at first meets the eye. The word 'science' originally meant simply 'knowledge'. If science can be seen as a search for knowledge based on an objective examination of evidence then history is as much of a science as physics or philosophy or literature. Secondly, the scientific approach is not totally empirical in character. Like history, physics or biology rely heavily on the systematic classification of data. Thirdly, scientists making judgements have to face the same moral and ethical dilemmas as historians. Finally, scientific laws are no longer considered to be as absolute and universal as they once were. Science has become as tentative in its conclusions as history. Perhaps Jacob Burckhardt was correct when he wrote that history 'is the most unscientific of all the sciences'.

(1) Assess the validity of E. H. Carr's distinction between art and science.
(2) Why do some historians attempt to find historical 'laws'?
(3) Should history be a science?
(4) In what ways does 'objectivity' for scientists and historians differ? Account for these differences.
(5) The past can never be objective but the historian can. Discuss.
(6) Was Burckhardt right?

History and the Social Sciences

History is not the only subject to deal with people in the past. All the social sciences deal with people not just in the present but in the past as well. But history differs from other disciplines in that it is concerned with events, with change and with the specific rather than the general. As G. R. Elton said: 'History treats fundamentally of the transformation of things (people, institutions, ideas and so on) from one state into another, and the event is its concern as well as its instrument.' But despite difference in method historians should not, cannot ignore the contributions made by other disciplines. This does not mean that the autonomy of history as a subject in its own right is being brought into question.

At a simple level history does provide, and has always done, much of the raw material for the social sciences – who can understand present Soviet thinking on defence without appreciating the historical circumstances which led to those attitudes? Yet perceptions by historians and social scientists of each other have not really got beyond the stereotypes of historians as undiscriminating 'fact-collectors' and social scientists as purveyors of jargon and general theory. Yet the gap between history and social science appears to have narrowed dramatically in the last thirty years. Quantitative history has become more important. There has been a shift among sociologists and economists to the problems of social and economic transition and development. Historians have become concerned to understand the 'mentalities' of past societies and to explore such matters as lunacy, crime, magic, customs, oppression and deviance, class-formation and domestic social relations. This has led to the widespread borrowing of categories between the disciplines and to some erosion of the boundaries between them.

There are undoubtedly many parallels between history and the social sciences. However, there are important differences. First, gross oversimplification though this may sound, the social sciences are concerned with the present while history is concerned with the past. Secondly, the social sciences are concerned with developing explanatory laws through an empirical methodology. Historians are concerned with reconstructing individual events in their uniqueness. In 1979 Anthony Giddens wrote that

What history is, or should be, cannot be analysed in separation from what the social sciences are, or should be. . . . There simply are no logical or even methodological distinctions between the social sciences and history.

and in 1982 Philip Abrams stated that

Sociological explanation is essentially historical . . . there is no essential difference between the sociologist and the historian.

History can tell us as much about structures, about individuals and their actions and about change and its effects upon ideas and people as sociology or politics or anthropology or psychology. Historians have applied the models, theories and methodologies of the social sciences to historical problems. This has been both successful and a failure. Economic models and computers have been used successfully to elucidate the past. Elite and class theories have been applied equally to first-century Roman history and to nineteenth-century Britain. The Annales school of French historians is the best exemplar of this synthesis of disciplines. Lucien Febvre and Marc Bloch, the founders, were influenced by Durkheimian notions of collective psychology. Bloch's *Feudal Society* and *French Rural History* are littered with interdisciplinary references. Their aspiration, and it has been made more explicit by later Annalistes such as Charles Morazé, Fernand Braudel and Emmanuel Le Roy Ladurie, was for a history that was more global or 'total' than the traditional approach. This holistic approach attempts to restore a sense of the essential unity of human experience, a process which works more successfully in small-scale studies like *Montaillou* than with the grandiose global studies of Braudel.

(1) Why should historians have an interdisciplinary outlook?

(2) Why have some historians placed great emphasis on the autonomy of history?

(3) Is 'total' history possible?

(4) How do social concepts like 'class' or 'élite' help the historian of early modern Europe?

(5) If historians want to explain the past as fully as possible they need to use the methodologies and concepts of other disciplines. Discuss.

History and the Environment

The relationship between people and their environment is of major social and political concern today. But its importance to history has long been recognised. The Greeks understood the close relationship between the development of the city states and their geographical environment. Immanuel Kant wrote in the late eighteenth century:

> Which was the first, history or geography? The latter provides the foundations for the former, because events always take place in a certain setting. History involves a continuous process of changing events; but material phenomena also change, and so result at certain periods in completely new geographies. Geography is thus the basis. As we recognise a history of a past period, so we must recognise the geography of a past period.

W. G. Hoskins would agree:

> (The geologist) explains to us the bones of the landscape, the fundamental structure that gives form and colour to the scene and produces a certain kind of topography and natural vegetation. But the flesh that covers the bones, and the details of the features, are the concern of the historian whose task it is to show how man has clothed the geological skeleton.

People are and have always been at the mercy of their environment. The more primitive the society and the more severe the physical conditions the more direct this relationship has been – take, for example, life in sixteenth-century England. Most of society, what has been called 'the submerged nine-tenths', was concerned with the production of food. But people can only produce the kind of crops that the soil and climate will allow. The open field system with an individual's strips spread across the large fields was the result of the community's desire to share different types of land fairly. That the open field system was not universal in England can be accounted for by soil and climate. This in turn can influence the organisation of both society and economy. Food, clothing, the material conditions of life, people's values and beliefs can all be shown to be a result of their response to the environment. Why had the peasantry died out as a social group by 1500 in England whereas they persisted in much of the rest of Europe until the late eighteenth and nineteenth centuries? Was it a consequence of the different geographies?

Though historians should be sceptical of the more extravagant environmentalists' theories – for example, that there is an association between outbreaks of industrial unrest with sunspot activity or that Halley's comet precedes disasters – the case for careful consideration of the natural environment is clearly made. But whether the environment determined the development of the past or whether it merely influenced it is open to question. Certainly Lucien Febvre favoured influence when he wrote that: 'There are no necessities, but everywhere possibilities; and man, as master of the possibilities, is the judge of their use.'

(1) 'History is governed by geography.' Discuss.
(2) How far has the environment influenced social organisation?
(3) How does an understanding of the past environment help historians to explain events? Base your answer on specific events you have studied.
(4) Why should the map be as important a source for historians as for the environmentalist?

History and Technology

It is difficult for historians to discuss possible paths of human development, particularly in the modern world, without focusing upon science and technology. The spectacular 'successes' like putting people on the moon, exploding the nuclear bomb, and developing new drugs have an obvious place in history. But a great deal of science and technology has been at a much less sophisticated level, though historically nonetheless important – take for example the development of the plough in Europe. The soil and climate of Mediterranean Europe led to the development of the 'scratch-plough' or 'aratrum' designed to break-up the surface of the soil to allow irrigation. This plough was unsuited to the heavier soils and wetter climate of northern Europe and consequently a different sort of plough, the 'carucca', emerged with a mould-board to turn the soils over. The difference in technology was a pragmatic response to different environmental conditions. No sophisticated theory here, only practical application.

Science may be taken to mean the advancement in peoples' understanding of the ways in which the observable world works. It is not surprising that science has long been closely related to religious beliefs and to asking questions of nature. Ancient Babylonian, Indian and Aztec religion demanded the accurate prediction of heavenly events and consequently their sciences were largely devoted to the study of astronomy. But they produced little or no technological spin-off in terms of inventions which either altered the landscape or improved the material life of people other than the prediction of solar events like eclipses for ritual purposes. Science could easily become dogma shrouded in mystery and change assiduously guarded against, as Galileo found to his cost. Science maintained the 'world-view' of those who controlled society.

The scientific revolution of the seventeenth century brought major changes in how an influential minority viewed the world. Newton united terrestrial and celestial views of motion in his theory of gravitation. There were advances in optics, hydraulics, mechanics, chemistry, biology and mathematics. Though they had practical implications they too had little real impact on the lives of most people. But this is definitely not true of the innovations of the century between 1750 and 1850. The 'industrial revolutions', first in Britain, then in Europe and the rest of the world, expanded productive capacity through the application of new technologies and energy sources often within the collective environment of the factory. Communication changed. Societies urbanised. Population expanded, liberated from the stranglehold of uncertain food supplies by changed agrarian techniques.

In the last century there has been a growth in the extent of scientific and technological knowledge as well as a change in the economic, social and ideological context within which scientific work operates. Science has yet again become of central concern to the state. It may have been shorn of its mystical character but the mystery and secrecy are still there. The issues about science which were raised in the past still persist: what sort of science do we want? How much of it do we want? Who should do it? How should they and their activities be controlled? How these are approached is ultimately the consequence of answers to only one question – what sort of society do we want? As John Osborne wrote in *Inadmissible Evidence*:

> I hereby swear and affirm. . . . My belief in . . . the technological revolution, the growing, pressing, urgent need for more and more scientists, for more and more schools and universities . . . the theme of change, realistic decisions based on a highly developed and professional study of society by people who really know their subject, the overdue need for us to adapt ourselves to different conditions, the theme and challenge of such rapid change, change, rapid change.

(1) Historical development is the result of scientific and technological change. Discuss.
(2) What part has history to play in modern technological society?
(3) Technological change has always been more important than purely scientific change. Do you agree?
(4) Assess the role of inventions in any period that you have studied.
(5) Examine and explain the relationship between science and religion.
(6) Understanding of science brings power. Understandably people with power want to retain the mystique of science. How valid is this assertion?

History and Culture

The development of 'total' history has led to historians beginning to look at the role of 'culture' in the past. Keith Thomas, Peter Burke and Alan Macfarlane have increased our understanding of 'popular' culture in the sixteenth and seventeenth centuries. Other historians have considered more recent events. Culture is, in general terms, an expression of social attitudes, language and ideology. Poetry, art, music, architecture, drama and literature generally have become much more important and legitimate avenues through which historians attempt to elucidate those attitudes. Some distinction can be drawn between the overall social culture, that which is the concern of all society and which contains the dominant social values – the Gramscian idea of 'hegemony' – and the various sub-cultures that exist within that hegemony and which colour a limited sector of activity within society. The relationship between the two is of major importance especially at the cultural interface where the two may come into conflict. Cultural attitudes within any society are the result of social position and can be an expression of antipathy to the culture of the ruling class.

In sixteenth-century England drama became a highly specific combination of acted dialogue between individuals and developed spectacle. Its origin lay in the popular rather than the aristocratic theatre. It drew upon the experience of pre-literate medieval culture. Acts of violence were now directly staged as opposed to being narrated. This form of drama as visible action drew directly on the simple form of dumb-show or the more highly staged processions and pageants. Within this synthesis of popular drama was added a more religious and humanist form of didactic dialogue which led to the dramatic speech and monologue. Within Shakespeare, for example, there are various speech-forms – those of war, politics, business, trade as well as 'vulgar' speech. By contrast the tendency in the seventeenth century was an increasing social exclusivity of the theatre beginning as early as 1610 with the general move to private theatres. This continued to the Civil War and was formally legislated for after the Restoration. Plays changed from public tragedy to heroic drama. Language became more formalised. Drama reflected the change in the nature of formal social attitudes.

(1) Why should an examination of 'culture' be important for historians?
(2) Examine either the development of literature or music and explain what light it sheds on any period you have studied.
(3) Which is more important for the historian, 'popular' or 'high' culture and why?
(4) How have cultural attitudes been transmitted in the past?

The Philosophy of History

In the thirteenth century the Arabian historian Ibn Khaldun wrote that:

> The inner meaning of history involves speculation and an attempt to get at the truth, subtle explanation of the causes and origins of existing things, and deep knowledge of the how and why of events. History therefore is firmly rooted in philosophy. It deserves to be accounted as a branch of philosophy.

Many historians are deeply sceptical of the philosophical basis of their subject. The reason lies in the nature of history as the study of unique events from which it is not possible to draw general laws. Models of the human past are consequently a delusion. That may well be true but it does not alter the value and insight which the application of theories to the past provide. One does not have to agree with Karl Marx or Max Weber to appreciate that their ideas do have importance for the historian. It makes their explanations and interpretations possible. Historians cannot escape theory.

(1) Why can historians not escape theory?
(2) What contribution has Marx made to the study of history?
(3) Theory provides frameworks but history provides the facts necessary to flesh out those frameworks. Discuss.
(4) There can never be historical laws. What is your reaction to this statement?

Bibliography

This list of books and articles falls into two groups: first, those on the nature of history and secondly, those concerned with study-skills. Those books marked * are more difficult.

1 The Nature of History

(a) Introductory

A. Marwick, *The Nature of History* (Macmillan, 2nd edn, 1981)
   A book written for the Open University as part of its independent learning course on Introduction to the Humanities.
A. Marwick *et al.*, *Introduction to History* (Open University, 1977)
J. Tosh, *The Pursuit of History* (Longman, 1984)
   An excellent, well-written study.

(b) Philosophy

* P. F. Atkinson, *Knowledge and Explanation in History* (Macmillan, 1977)
M. Bloch, *The Historian's Craft* (Manchester, 1954)
E. H. Carr, *What is History?* (Penguin, 1964, 2nd edn, 1987)
   Don't be misled by its seemingly simple approach.
G. R. Elton, *The Practice of History* (Fontana, 1969)
   A critique of Carr.
G. Kitson Clark, *The Critical Historian* (Heinemann, 1967)
* G. Leff, *History and Social Theory* (Merlin, 1969)
   A very readable study.
M. Stanford, *The Nature of Historical Knowledge* (Basil Blackwell, 1986)
   A very readable study of the problems of using sources, and much else besides.
* W. H. Walsh, *An Introduction to the Philosophy of History* (Hutchinson, 3rd edn, 1967)

(c) Approaches through historians

J. Cannon (ed.), *The Historian at Work* (Allen & Unwin, 1980)
   A good introduction to the work of several modern historians.

* J. Hexter, *On Historians* (Collins, 1979)
    Containing interesting critiques of Hill and Braudel.
F. Stern (ed.), *The Varieties of History* (Macmillan, 1970)
    Traces the development of historical consciousness through the writings
    of leading historians from 1700.

(d) Interdisciplinary approaches

* P. Abrams, *Historical Sociology* (Open Books, 1982)
    A difficult but very rewarding book.
P. Burke, *Sociology and History* (Allen & Unwin, 1980)
    A briefer and much less searching book.
R. Floud, *An Introduction to Quantitative Methods for Historians* (Methuen, 2nd
edn, 1979)
    The best introduction to the subject.
* G. F. Hawke, *Economics for Historians* (Cambridge, 1978)
W. G. Hoskins, *Local History in England* (Longman, 2nd edn, 1972)
    The work from which all local historians began.
S. C. Humphreys 'Reading History: History and Anthropology', *History
Today* (July 1984)
A. Rogers, *Approaches to Local History* (Longman, 2dn edn, 1978)
    An excellent introduction to the subject and the sources.
A. Seddon and J. Pappworth, *By Word of Mouth* (Methuen, 1983)
P. Thompson, *The Voice of the Past: Oral History* (Oxford University Press,
1978)
The Times Atlas of *World History*, ed. G. Barraclough (Times Books, revised
edn, 1984)

(d) What is History?

There is an excellent, accessible and continuing series of articles in *History
Today* on the different types of history.
C. Abel *et al.*, 'What is Third World History?' (September 1985)
C. Brooke *et al.*, 'What is Religious History?' (August 1985)
D. C. Coleman *et al.*, 'What is Economic History?' (February 1985)
R. Cooter *et al.*, 'What is the History of Science?' (April 1985)
M. Howard *et al.*, 'What is Military History?' (January 1985)
O. Hufton *et al.*, 'What is Women's History?' (June 1985)
P. Mettam *et al.*, 'What is History? The Great Debate' (May 1984)
J. Pickstone *et al.*, 'What is the History of Science?' (May 1985)
R. Samuel *et al.*, 'What is Social History?' (March 1985)
D. C. Watt *et al.*, 'What is Diplomatic History?' (July 1985)
T. P. Wiseman *et al.*, 'What is Political History?' (January 1985)

These have been collected in J. Gardiner (ed.), *What is History Today* (Macmillan, 1988)

2 Study-skills

R. Barrass, *Study! A Guide to Effective Study, Revision and Examination Techniques* (Chapman & Hall, 1984)
T. Buzan, *Make the Most of Your Mind* (Pan, 1977)
T. Buzan, *Use your Head* (BBC, revised edn, 1982)
H. Maddox, *How to Study* (Pan, 1980 edn)
L. A. Marshall and F. Rowland, *A Guide to Learning Independently* (Open University Press, 1983)
R. Palmer and C. Pope, *Brain Train: Studying for Success* (Spon, 1984)
    The only book with a chapter on the use of the computer in study-skills.
D. Rowntree, *Learn How to Study* (Macdonald, 1976)